Growing Up

A CLASSIC AMERICAN

CHILDHOOD

Clockwise from left: *Marina vos Savant (Mom),
Joseph Mach (Dad), Marilyn vos Savant,
Joe Mach (brother), Bob Mach (brother)*

Growing Up

A CLASSIC AMERICAN CHILDHOOD

WHAT KIDS SHOULD KNOW
BEFORE THEY LEAVE HOME

Marilyn vos Savant

W. W. NORTON & COMPANY

NEW YORK LONDON

For information about permission to reproduce selections from this book, write to
Permissions, W. W. Norton & Company, Inc., 500 Fifth Avenue, New York, NY 10110

The text of this book is composed in Garamond with the display set in Archway Script
Composition by Carole Desnoes
Manufacturing by R. R. Donnelly & Sons, Inc.
Book design by Jo Anne Metsch
Production manager: Amanda Morrison

Library of Congress Cataloging-in-Publication Data

Vos Savant, Marilyn, date.
Growing up : a classic American childhood / Marilyn vos Savant.
p. cm.
Includes bibliographical references.
ISBN 0-393-05125-0
1. Child rearing—United States. 2. Parenting—United States. 3. Children—United
States—Conduct of life. 4. Teenagers—United States—Conduct of life. I. Title.

HQ769 .V637 2002
649'.1'0973—dc21   2002022840

W. W. Norton & Company, Inc., 500 Fifth Avenue, New York, N.Y. 10110
www.wwnorton.com

W. W. Norton & Company Ltd., Castle House, 75/76 Wells Street, London W1T 3QT

1 2 3 4 5 6 7 8 9 0

To my daughter, Mary,
and her husband, David,
and to their newborn twin girls,
Michelle and Valerie

ALSO BY MARILYN VOS SAVANT

Ask Marilyn

More Marilyn

The World's Most Famous Math Problem:
The Proof of Fermat's Last Theorem
and Other Mathematical Mysteries

"I've Forgotten Everything I Learned in School":
A Refresher Course to Help You
Reclaim Your Education

Of Course I'm for Monogamy:
I'm Also for Everlasting Peace and
an End to Taxes

The Power of Logical Thinking

The Art of Spelling:
The Madness and the Method

Acknowledgments

I would like to thank Stephanie Gayle, whose degree in American Studies and English Literature from Smith College served her well throughout this project. As my editorial assistant and researcher, Stephanie worked tirelessly to put together this book from start to finish, gathering suggestions from *Parade* readers all across the country and researching countless organizations for our list of resources. She was a great source of inspiration as well as a sounding board for my own ideas.

I also would like to thank Bevin Butler, my favorite Brown University student, who is finishing her degree in the history of art and architecture this year. During summer break, Bevin pored through our favorite archives in search of just the right photos, a process that amused and delighted us all, especially during our regular photo meetings, when we voted on our choices. (My vote always counted most: no surprise there!)

I also would like to thank Sara Brzowsky, editor of the "Ask Marilyn" column, who generously provided her services over many a weekend to edit this book. With great intelligence and good cheer, Sara pored over every line, offering the wisdom of her twenty years of experience at *Parade* and enhancing my ability to serve my readers well. A single mother by choice, her son Jacob is one lucky youngster to be growing up in her care.

Contents

INTRODUCTION / 11

1 AMERICAN HERITAGE AND OTHER CULTURES / 15

2 FAMILY, FRIENDS, AND NEIGHBORS / 21

3 LOVING AND CARING FOR OTHERS / 27

4 INDOOR AND BACKYARD FUN / 33

5 ART AND BEAUTY IN OUR LIVES / 39

6 COOKING WITH DELIGHT / 45

7 HOUSEHOLD CLEANING AND LAUNDRY / 51

8 HOME REPAIR / 57

9 TELEPHONES AND TALKING / 63

10 THE ART OF COMMUNICATION / 69

11 DATING AND DINING / 75

12 ETIQUETTE AND NICE THINGS TO KNOW / 81

13 KEEPING CLEAN, NEAT, AND HEALTHY / 87

14 CURING WHAT AILS YOU / 93

15 EXERCISE AND THE SPORTING LIFE / 99

16 ENJOYING THE GREAT OUTDOORS / 105

10 *Contents*

17 PLANTS AND TREES / 111

18 ANIMALS IN OUR WORLD / 117

19 SCIENCE ALL AROUND US / 123

20 SAFETY IN AN EMERGENCY / 129

21 NAVIGATING IN OUR WORLD / 135

22 AUTOMOBILE HANDLING AND CARE / 141

23 HOME AND OFFICE EQUIPMENT / 147

24 ORGANIZING YOUR LIFE / 153

25 MEDICAL KNOWLEDGE / 159

26 CONSUMER AND SHOPPING SKILLS / 165

27 DESIGNING AND BUILDING / 171

28 BUSINESS AND FREE ENTERPRISE / 177

29 MANAGING YOUR MONEY / 183

30 CRITICAL THINKING SKILLS / 189

31 PREPARING FOR THE FUTURE / 195

32 BEING A GOOD CITIZEN / 201

RESOURCES / 207

Introduction

Welcome to the world of childhood and youth, once again. It was—and still is—a time of joy, exhilaration, confusion, and dismay. Do you ever wish you could go back to those days and live them all over again? You don't?! (And no wonder.) Then at least you can try to make that time a perfect world for someone else, as perfect as you are able. This book makes a thoroughly loving effort to serve as a family guide to a classic American childhood. It's the childhood we all wanted for ourselves and never quite experienced, although we knew it existed just around the corner, in books and movies, as well as in our own homes at special moments and so often on weekend mornings.

Scan the chapter titles, and you'll see that we cover the territory from hopscotch to career choices and just about everything in between. Some chapters (such as "Indoor and Backyard Fun") are naturally younger than most, and other chapters (such as "Automobile Handling and Care") are older, of course. But each chapter in itself ranges throughout the elementary and high school years. For instance, the chapter called "Managing Your Money" starts with piggy banks and ends with credit cards.

In general, two kinds of activities are included: the sort of experience that kids should have at least once in their lives and the sort of practical skill that all kids should have before they leave home. Take the chapter called "American Heritage and Other Cultures" as an example. It would be ideal if, by age eighteen, you were to: "Have drawn your name in the air with a sparkler on the Fourth of July" (meaning: at least once in your life) and "Be able to draw an outline of your community and locate your house on it" (meaning: before you leave home). Schoolwork (like knowing multiplication and division tables) is not included.

One important note: this book was written for *all* kids, parents, and grandparents, not just those in traditional families, complete with Mom playing the piano, Brother and Sister singing along, and Dad smiling fondly, plus a golden retriever under the bed on stormy nights. We all know those people aren't real. Instead, American life encompasses a wide variety of situations, from adopted kids to blended families to mothers or fathers living happily on their own. No one can live an ideal life because the world is not ideal. But we all can *aspire* to perfection. That is what makes each superior violinist and gymnast and artist unique: doing our best in our own inimitable way. So, readers, be sure to apply—or adapt—each item in the chapters to your own situation. (Example: you don't have a brother who annoys you? Then how about the boy next door?) Remember: the freedom to be an individual is the essence of America.

Using this book as a guide, you can give your kids (or grandkids) the kind of classic American childhood experiences and practical skills that will keep them looking back fondly and help prepare them to take their place in the world.

And whatever you do, wherever you go, all of you: please don't forget to write. I'm always happy to hear from you at marilyn@parade.com.

Marilyn vos Savant

Growing Up

A CLASSIC AMERICAN

CHILDHOOD

AMERICAN HERITAGE AND OTHER CULTURES

In America, anyone can become president.
That's one of the risks you take.

—*Adlai Stevenson (1900–1965)*
U.S. political leader, diplomat

1

American Heritage and Other Cultures

IT WOULD BE IDEAL IF, BY AGE EIGHTEEN, YOU WERE TO:

❑ Have drawn your name in the air with a sparkler on the Fourth of July.

❑ Have gone trick-or-treating on Halloween, in costume, with your friends.

❑ Have attended a Thanksgiving Day parade and waved an American flag.

❑ Be able to draw an outline of your own state and locate the major cities and rivers on it.

❑ Be able to recognize your state flag and identify your state motto, bird, flower, and tree.

❑ Have attended a state or regional fair, sampled many foods, and taken part in the activities.

❑ Know why and how your own town or city was founded and by whom.

❑ Be able to draw an outline of your community and locate your house on it.

❑ Have talked with an elderly resident and asked about all the changes that have occurred in the community over the decades.

❑ Have taken at least one walking tour of your town, the longer and more often, the better.

❑ Have visited all the major points of both historical interest and modern interest in your town.

❑ Have visited the inside of the oldest building in your town, if possible, and read about its history.

❑ Have visited the oldest business in town, asked about its history, and visited any archive or museum that might be on the premises.

❑ Have volunteered to work at a local historical-preservation society.

❑ Have taken a long walk on a local historic trail and felt just a little like a time traveler.

❑ Have visited your town's City Hall and as many other public buildings as possible.

❑ Have visited your state capital and walked through as many of the public buildings as you were allowed to go inside.

❑ Have recited aloud (and alone) at least one famous American speech.

❑ Know the words to the United States Pledge of Allegiance.

❑ Know the words to *The Star-Spangled Banner.* No one can sing it well!

❑ Have watched an American flag being raised, lowered, and folded.

❑ Have visited an American history museum and are able to identify Early American furniture.

❑ Have read an American newspaper that is at least a hundred years old, plus a newspaper from each decade since then, especially those published during historic times.

❑ Be able to name some historic Native American leaders and say why they are famous.

❑ Have attended a truly American cultural event, such as a Native American festival or a rodeo.

❑ Have tried square dancing—at least long enough to no longer feel silly and begin to have fun.

❑ Have visited an authentic ghost town and seen Mount Rushmore.

❑ Have visited the Grand Canyon or another stunning and distinctive American landscape feature.

❑ Have driven across our vast, glorious country to appreciate its great beauty and amazing diversity.

❑ Have visited Washington, D.C., seen the White House, and toured as many public buildings as possible.

❑ Have read the memoirs of at least one American president from the early days of our country.

❑ Be able to name all the branches of the armed forces and describe what they do and where.

❑ Have visited the site of a Civil War battlefield and thought about the events that took place.

❑ Have visited your largest local war memorial and read the names inscribed there until you felt humbled by their sacrifice.

❑ Have spoken with some veterans of foreign wars and asked about their experiences overseas.

❑ Have visited the Statue of Liberty in New York Harbor and spent time at the museum there.

❏ Have visited Ellis Island and walked along the same halls that so many immigrants passed through.

❏ Have made friends with people from a few different foreign countries.

❏ Have attended a few cultural-heritage street festivals held in your town and tried all kinds of food.

❏ Know about your own ethnic heritage, at least going back a couple of generations.

❏ Have spent time with a gorgeous picture book about each of your own ethnic heritages.

❏ Have visited the United Nations in New York City and learned about what it does.

❏ Have visited some famous American skyscrapers, starting with the oldest, and watched them grow higher as the decades went by.

❏ Have planned a typical "American" itinerary for a visitor from a foreign country to introduce him or her to our way of life.

EXTRA CREDIT

Have attended a reenactment of a historic American battle or other event.

FAMILY, FRIENDS, AND NEIGHBORS

The simplest toy, one which even the youngest child
can operate, is called a grandparent.

—*Samuel Levenson (1911–1980)*
American humorist, television personality

2

Family, Friends, and Neighbors

IT WOULD BE IDEAL IF, BY AGE EIGHTEEN, YOU WERE TO:

❑ Have learned to tie your brother's necktie, if you're female. Fathers and grandfathers count, too.

❑ Have learned to braid your sister's hair, even if you're male. Cousins and mothers count, too.

❑ Have learned how to pin your mother's or sister's brooch straight, especially if you're a male.

❑ Have watched your father shave, especially when he's getting ready to go out with your mother.

❑ Have watched your mother apply makeup, especially when she's dressing to go out with your father.

❑ Have helped your parents get dressed for a special event, including inserting your father's cufflinks and fastening your mother's jewelry.

❑ Have gone on separate weekend vacations alone with your mother and father.

❑ Have gone on an all-day picnic with your whole family, making all the food yourselves.

❑ Have attended a carnival (or gone to an amusement park) with your whole family and watched your father try to win a prize for your mother.

❑ Have gone with your whole family to an old-fashioned circus, the kind that takes place in a tent.

❑ Have posed for an inexpensive professional family photo every year, regardless of whether you were embarrassed about the last one.

❑ Have marked your height inside the closet door where you keep your clothes.

❑ Have spent a week with each of your grandparents at least once, preferably alone.

❑ Have asked each of your grandparents to tell you as much as he or she could remember about your parents as children.

❑ Have offered to help each of your grandparents create an album with their loose photos.

❑ Have offered to explore the contents of the attic of each of your grandparents.

❑ Have tried the favorite recreational activity of each one of your grandparents, preferably with him or her along to serve as an instructor, guide, or coach.

❑ Know the first and last names of everyone in your family going back three generations.

❑ Have tried to discover the origin and meaning of both your father's and mother's surnames.

❑ Have attended a family reunion, the kind where people arrive from all over the country.

❑ Be able to cite three good qualities of every relative or acquaintance that you dislike.

❑ Be able to state the age, height, and weight of each of your parents and grandparents and know their birthdates, how long they've been married, and the dates of their wedding anniversaries.

❑ Be able to state exactly what your parents and grandparents do at work (or at home) each day, including routine responsibilities and important ones.

❑ Be able to name all of the friends of your parents and state what they do for a living.

❑ Be able to state the age, height, and approximate weight of each of your brothers and sisters and know their birthdates, their special interests, how well they perform in school, and their plans for the future.

❑ Be able to name all of the friends of your brothers and sisters and state the activities they usually enjoy together, how well the friends perform in school, and their plans for the future.

❑ Be comfortable saying, "I love you," to a relative or close friend, but only if and when you really mean it.

❑ Be able to confide your innermost secrets to your mother and your innermost fears to your father.

❑ Be able to have both male and female friends, regardless of whether you're a male or female yourself.

❑ Have attended a pajama party with your friends, the kind of party where you talk all night instead of sleeping.

❑ Have planned a surprise party for a friend so well that it actually turned out to be a surprise.

❏ Have tried switching places with a friend, each of you spending a day with the other's family.

❏ Have fostered a friendship between two acquaintances who possess common interests.

❏ Have met all the people in your neighborhood and tried to make a few special friends among the adults.

❏ Have made an effort to meet the new kids on the block— adults included—when they moved into your neighborhood.

❏ Have organized or participated in a block party so that everyone could get to know each other.

❏ Have a set of household chores that you routinely complete, whether you get paid for doing them or not.

❏ Have participated in keeping a family scrapbook with photos and souvenirs of special events.

❏ Have tried writing in a journal for a few weeks to see if you'd like to keep one routinely.

EXTRA CREDIT

Be able to tell your family if you're gay.

LOVING AND CARING FOR OTHERS

We are here on Earth to do good to others.
What the others are here for, I don't know.

—*W. H. Auden (1907–1973)*
English poet

3

Loving and Caring for Others

IT WOULD BE IDEAL IF, BY AGE EIGHTEEN, YOU WERE TO:

❑ Have offered to help a mother in the neighborhood with her newborn baby, especially if she has other young children.

❑ Have held a baby under a month old, spoken to him gently, and tried to make him smile.

❑ Have fed a baby under six months old, including offering her solid food and giving her a bottle.

❑ Have changed a diaper and asked the parents how often this little chore must be repeated daily.

❑ Have successfully quieted a crying baby under a year old by cradling and soothing him or her.

❑ Have helped a parent bathe and dress a small child under the age of two or three years.

❑ Know half a dozen nursery rhymes, stories, and songs for little children by heart.

❑ Have baby-sat for both boys and girls ranging in age from six months to six years.

❑ Have offered to help out at a day-care facility for children whose mothers work.

❑ Have volunteered to visit hospitals and spend time with children who are ill or injured and alone or whose relatives are unable to visit them enough.

❑ Have volunteered to work as a candy striper at a nearby hospital.

❑ Have successfully encouraged a friend or relative to get the medical attention he or she needed but was afraid to seek.

❑ Have visited your friends and relatives in the hospital, even if you are afraid to see them ill or injured—but only if they want you to visit.

❑ Have volunteered to spend a few days or evenings with an adult relative who has just returned home from the hospital and who has no family in residence.

❑ Know the most helpful things to do for an adult who is sick and recovering.

❑ Know how to be of aid and comfort to a person who will never be well again.

❏ Have volunteered to spend a few days or evenings with an adult relative who is grieving for a departed loved one.

❏ Have visited a nursing home and spent time with those residents who have no relatives left or whose relatives don't visit them often.

❏ Have gone back to that same nursing home several times and spent more time with the same people.

❏ Have volunteered to teach computer skills to the elderly people in your neighborhood, and when they resisted, managed to talk them into it, regardless.

❏ Have continued to provide technical support to all the elderly people in your neighborhood who are now online and loving it.

❏ Know how to aid elderly or handicapped persons in public without seeming superior.

❏ Have volunteered your services to a person with a disability who could use help with a certain chore on a routine basis.

❏ Know what to do (and what not to do) if you discover a person in immediate need of help.

❏ Have volunteered to work at an organization that provides assistance to people in difficult circumstances.

❑ Have donated money or goods to a charitable organization that helps people who are poor.

❑ Have volunteered to work for a literacy organization.

❑ Have volunteered to help teach English as a second language to people new to this country.

❑ Have volunteered to work for an organization that helps immigrants settle into their communities.

❑ Have volunteered at your school to help transfer students adjust to their new surroundings.

❑ Have visited an animal shelter and inquired about what sorts of animals are handled there.

❑ Have volunteered to work at an animal shelter but not taken any animals home afterward.

❑ Have written a love letter to your dog or cat and read it aloud to him or her.

❑ Have cared for a dog or cat, including when it's sick. Forget trying to give a cat a pill.

❑ Have groomed a dog and given him or her a bath. Forget trying to bathe and groom a cat.

❑ Have taught your dog to obey but not to do tricks that compromise his dignity as your friend.

❑ Have learned to obey your cat and feed him or her as desired. Nothing else may be possible.

❑ Know what to do (and what not to do) when a dog or cat (even your own pet) has been injured.

❑ Have prepared a set of instructions that a home pet-sitter can use to care for your dog or cat.

❑ Have maintained a fresh-water aquarium with a variety of fish and plants and other creatures.

❑ Have volunteered to house-sit, pet-sit, or plant-sit for a neighbor leaving for a vacation.

EXTRA CREDIT

Have "adopted" an elderly person who is alone and
added him or her to your extended family,
especially on holidays.

INDOOR AND BACKYARD FUN

Learning how to knit was a snap. It was learning how
to stop that nearly destroyed me.

—Erma Bombeck (1927–1996)
American newspaper columnist, humorist

4

Indoor and Backyard Fun

IT WOULD BE IDEAL IF, BY AGE EIGHTEEN, YOU WERE TO:

❑ Have played jacks, shot marbles, and performed at least one impressive yo-yo maneuver.

❑ Have played a singing and clapping game, such as "Take Me Out to the Ball Game."

❑ Have played follow-the-leader, tag, hide-and-seek, red rover, and capture-the-flag.

❑ Have played games that require following instructions rapidly, such as "Simon Says."

❑ Have played hopscotch on a pattern that you drew with chalk on a sidewalk or driveway.

❑ Have swung without being pushed and tried to balance just right on a seesaw with a friend.

❑ Have walked on stilts and bounced all over the sidewalk or driveway on a pogo stick.

❑ Have skipped rope, both holding the rope yourself and with two friends holding the ends.

❑ Have chosen sides for friends by using a rhyming device such as "Eenie Meenie Minie Moe."

❑ Have tried spinning a Hula Hoop® around your waist, if only to appreciate what your parents and grandparents knew how to do so well.

❑ Have played so much with various Nerf® balls that you were thrown out of the house to continue playing outdoors.

❑ Have thrown a Frisbee® so much that it eventually landed somewhere inaccessible, even to you.

❑ Have played Wiffle® ball with friends and batted the ball so successfully that it broke.

❑ Have had plenty of squirt-gun fights, but only with the small variety: no automatic weapons!

❑ Have made your own bubble mix using liquid detergent (and water) and blown soap bubbles.

❑ Be able to blow really big bubbles with chewing gum, a skill that should never be lost!

❑ Have made your own play dough and used it to make impressions of your hands and feet.

❑ Have used blank paper to cut out a string of paper dolls that hold hands with each other.

❑ Have created balloon animals on your own without the aid of an instruction booklet.

❑ Have made hand puppets from old socks and staged an impromptu show with a friend.

❑ Have stayed overnight with a friend and made shadow puppets before you went to sleep.

❑ Have built a house of cards that became huge and then removed one card from the bottom layer.

❑ Have tried to perform a few simple magic tricks, even if you weren't quite convincing.

❑ Have spent an afternoon creating an "unbreakable" secret code for you and your best friend to use when writing notes to each other.

❑ Have played games that require only pencil and paper, such as hangman, with friends.

❑ Have played board games with friends, family, and adults who didn't try to let you win.

❑ Have played card games that mix luck and skill with people of your own experience level.

❑ Have learned an adult game (like bridge or chess) that you can play with friends for life.

❑ Have played charades enough so that you lost your feeling of self-consciousness and had fun.

❑ Have gone on a scavenger hunt that sent you and your friends all over the neighborhood.

❑ Have made simple paper airplanes that really flew without using any kind of instructions.

❑ Have put together a little boat that actually sailed in the bathtub or a pond without using a kit.

❑ Have put together a complicated model, such as a sailing ship or a replica of the human body.

❑ Have learned an arts or craft activity that you can follow alone for life, getting better and better at it over the years. Don't be concerned about your skill level now.

❑ Have worked crossword puzzles successfully and tried to improve your proficiency level.

❑ Have spent a day indoors alone with yourself, working

with your hands, with no distractions whatsoever: no radio, no television, and no music playing in the background.

❑ Have spent a day outdoors alone, working in the yard, again with nothing to accompany your thoughts and feelings.

❑ Have completed a jigsaw puzzle of more than one thousand pieces by yourself, with only soft music playing in the background.

❑ Have played "statues" in your room with an overnight friend and—when someone in the house needed quiet (like at six o'clock on Saturday morning)—done your best not to be caught moving.

❑ Have read at least a dozen novels of your own choosing that weren't assigned in school.

EXTRA CREDIT

Have stood in the spray of a fire hydrant that was opened for hot neighborhood kids by a friendly firefighter.

ART AND BEAUTY IN OUR LIVES

I saw the play under the worst circumstances: the curtain was up.

—George S. Kaufman (1899–1961)
American playwright, radio personality, humorist

5

Art and Beauty in Our Lives

IT WOULD BE IDEAL IF, BY AGE EIGHTEEN, YOU WERE TO:

❑ Have heard classical music played by an orchestra in a major concert hall.

❑ Have chosen your three favorite major classical composers, at least for now.

❑ Have listened to the ABCs of grand opera: *Aïda, La Bohème,* and *Carmen.*

❑ Have visited a major classical art museum and walked slowly through every room.

❑ Have chosen your favorite dozen pieces of classical artwork, including painting and sculpture. Be sure to ignore both critical and popular opinion.

❑ Have visited a major modern art museum and left no item unnoticed, if not explored.

❑ Have chosen your favorite pieces of modern art and tried

to recreate a small version of one of them at home, if only to prove to yourself that it's harder than it looks.

❑ Be able to articulate why you like or don't like a piece of art or a whole school of art.

❑ Have participated in a window-painting contest, such as the kind offered by local merchants at Halloween.

❑ Have participated in a poster contest in which you displayed your originality and ingenuity with design.

❑ Have sat in front of a mirror and tried mightily (for at least an hour) to draw your own portrait in pencil.

❑ Have sat at your kitchen table and drawn a still life of whatever fresh fruit or vegetables happened to be at hand.

❑ Have tried painting an unchanging outdoor scene, such as your backyard, with watercolors.

❑ Have chosen your favorite keyboard instrument and tried to plink out a tune on it.

❑ Have chosen your favorite stringed instrument and tried to play a few notes.

❑ Have chosen your favorite percussion instrument and banged away until you were stopped.

❏ Have chosen your favorite wind instrument and tried hard to make it sound at all.

❏ Be able to identify all your favorite instruments when you hear them on the radio.

❏ Know the names of past and current artists who are most famous for playing those instruments.

❏ Have been a member of any kind of singing group, such as a school or church choir, even if you couldn't sing very well.

❏ Have enough confidence to sing aloud (alone) now and then, even if others might hear you.

❏ Have tried to learn how to whistle a tune, and—if you succeeded—delight passersby by whistling while you walk along the sidewalk.

❏ Have tried playing a harmonica, if only to achieve a sense of humility.

❏ Know how to play a musical instrument well enough to enjoy playing in a group.

❏ Have attended the three ballets *Cinderella, The Nutcracker,* and *The Sleeping Beauty* as a child—or at least watched them on television.

❑ Have attended the ballet
Swan Lake as a teenager
and not rooted for the
evil twin.

❑ Be able to waltz, fox-trot,
lindy, and do at least one
Latin dance. You'll be
thankful someday.

❑ Be able to dance the most popular current dances just
enough to have fun at parties.

❑ Have attended a musical play as a child, including the
kind written for children.

❑ Have attended a musical play as a teenager, including
operettas and modern classics.

❑ Have attended a Broadway production, including traveling
productions, of a serious play.

❑ Have watched a play by Shakespeare that was made into a
movie, but only one with great actors.

❑ Have been a character in a play, no matter how small:
including animals, vegetables, and minerals.

❑ Have seen at least one movie from every decade since
1910, including your parents' favorites.

❑ Have chosen your three favorite short poems and are able to recite them from memory.

❑ Have kept a scrapbook with anything that seemed special at the time, including clippings.

❑ Have shot, as a child, a roll of film or taken digital photos of each grandparent who lives nearby.

❑ Have shot, as a teenager, a roll of film or taken digital photos of a child, not including relatives.

❑ Have kept a photo album with the best film prints you've either received or shot on your own.

❑ Be able to draw an illustration at least well enough to get your point across to another person.

❑ Have written your own definition of art and discussed it with your family and friends.

EXTRA CREDIT

Be able to identify the major voice ranges: tenor, baritone, and bass for men; soprano, mezzo-soprano, and alto for women.

COOKING WITH DELIGHT

It's so beautifully arranged on the plate—you know someone's
fingers have been all over it.

—Julia Child, on nouvelle cuisine (1912–)
American chef, television personality

6

Cooking with Delight

IT WOULD BE IDEAL IF, BY AGE EIGHTEEN, YOU WERE TO:

❑ Be able to cook (not just open and pour!) a traditional breakfast, lunch, and dinner.

❑ Have cooked and served breakfast in bed for your parents on special occasions.

❑ Be able to set a table so that you feel like you're dining, not just sitting and eating.

❑ Be able to blow out a dinner candle without sending wax flying across the table.

❑ Be able to follow a recipe, including not skipping time-consuming steps or leaving out ingredients that you don't happen to have handy, and knowing when you can substitute ingredients that are more to your liking.

❑ Own a cooking dictionary so that you don't inadvertently fry when you should sauté, scald, sear, or simmer.

❑ Have made a big pot of soup from scratch, using your favorite ingredients and herbs.

❑ Have baked a loaf of bread (using yeast) without a bread machine.

❑ Have baked giant pretzels from scratch, salty or not, but at least soft and warm.

❑ Have baked a layer cake, including the frosting, without any packaged mixes.

❑ Have baked an apple pie, starting with fresh apples, without a mix or a premade pie shell.

❑ Have made old-fashioned chocolate fudge, the kind that forms a ball in cold water when it's ready.

❑ Have participated in an authentic taffy pull with your friends or relatives and not eaten too much afterward.

❑ Have made a gingerbread house without a kit, frosted it, and decorated it with candies.

❑ Have helped your parents cook a complete Thanksgiving or other special holiday dinner.

❑ Be able to cut, peel, and section all kinds of fruit, when appropriate, so that the result is both tasty and attractive.

❑ Know how to garnish food so that it is more appealing to the eye and even more flavorful than before.

❑ Have tried making your own salad dressing and worked on the result until it became your favorite.

❑ Be able to carve a turkey, ham, or roast without the result looking like jackals visited the table.

❑ Be able to brew really good coffee and tea, even if you don't drink them yourself.

❑ Have watched the people at your local coffeehouse make espresso and cappuccino.

❑ Be able to crack an egg and fry it without making a mess or breaking the yolk.

❑ Be able to boil an egg so that the shell can be removed in fewer than a million pieces.

❑ Be able to work with hot pots and pans without burning yourself and know how to handle a grease fire in a skillet before it happens for the first time.

❑ Be able to slice, dice, and rice without trips to the emergency room. Hint: use sharp knives.

❑ Be able to pop corn in any kind of popper, including a plain old pot and lid, and still enjoy the result: each popping method produces a different flavor.

❏ Know which kitchen appliances perform what functions and be able to operate them safely.

❏ Be able to open a tight (twist) lid on a jar or bottle and pop open bottle and jar tops that don't twist off.

❏ Know how to prevent sticky food containers (such as syrup bottles) from becoming glued shut.

❏ Know how to store nonperishable food items so that they retain their flavor longer.

❏ Know how to store perishable food items, including what to freeze, what not to freeze, and for how long.

❏ Know how to keep food either cold enough or hot enough for safety, both before and after cooking.

❏ Know how to heat leftovers with both an oven and a microwave, which method of heating is best for what foods, and why.

❏ Know when to discard leftovers and the health risks associated with undercooking food.

❏ Have planned a week of menus for your family and made a complete grocery list for it.

❏ Have cooked a complete lunch or dinner outdoors, either over a grill or over a campfire.

❏ Be able to put together a creative dinner in difficult circumstances, such as with few ingredients.

❏ Have taken a specialty cooking class (or watched a few programs on television) for a favorite type of food, such as pasta or dessert.

❏ Have spent time smelling and tasting various herbs and spices in order to learn about them.

❏ Have started with a basic recipe, then developed a unique recipe of your own from it—the more complex, the better.

❏ Have started a recipe file, including favorites from your parents and grandparents.

EXTRA CREDIT

Have created a gift basket of homemade food items for a relative who needs special attention for some reason, such as a recent disappointment or misfortune.

HOUSEHOLD CLEANING AND LAUNDRY

It's a small world, but not if you have to clean it.

—*Barbara Kruger (1945–)*
American artist

7

*Household Cleaning
and Laundry*

IT WOULD BE IDEAL IF, BY AGE EIGHTEEN, YOU WERE TO:

❑ Have cleaned your own bedroom from wall to wall,
   including the closet and under the bed.

❑ Have changed your own bed linen and learned how to
   make your bed neatly and quickly.

❑ Have dusted and polished the furniture in the living room,
   dining room, and any other common area, such as an
   entry hallway or a family room.

❑ Be able to use a vacuum cleaner, including changing the
   bag, replacing the belt, and cleaning the rollers.

❑ Be able to sweep, mop, wax, and polish most floor
   surfaces, including wood and tile, without damaging them.

❑ Have cleaned a kitchen thoroughly, including the oven
   and refrigerator, and even the walls.

❑ Know how to clean a toaster, a blender, and an electric can opener both thoroughly and safely.

❑ Be able to polish silver, copper and brass, and to clean crystal, including any chandeliers in the house.

❑ Be able to wash and dry dishes by hand and not take forever or break anything.

❑ Be able to wash and dry pots and pans and any other cooking paraphernalia efficiently.

❑ Be able to load and wash dishes in an automatic dishwasher so that nothing goes wrong.

❑ Know what you can grind safely and sensibly in an automatic garbage disposal in the sink.

❑ Know how to fix a jam in the garbage disposal when you make the inevitable mistake.

❑ Have cleaned a bathroom, including the walls, floor, bathtub, sink, commode, and mirror.

❑ Know how and when to use antibacterials, such as disinfectants and antiseptics, and the dangers of overuse.

❑ Have washed both windows and mirrors in such a way that they didn't streak in the sunlight from any angle.

❑ Know which cleaning agents are dangerous to mix. In general, to be safe, don't mix anything at all.

❑ Know which cleaning agents can damage which surfaces or have fumes that are dangerous for you or your pets. For example, even housepaint fumes can kill tropical fish.

❑ Know how to get rid of vermin, insects, and other pests without endangering children or your pets.

❑ Know what moths can do and how to prevent an infestation, other than using repellent, which often smells funny.

❑ Know how to spot-clean a carpet or rug without causing damage, such as removing the color.

❑ Know how (and when) to spot-clean your clothes without turning a spot into a stain, instead.

❑ Know how to read clothing labels so that you can care for your clothes properly.

❑ Know which clothes should be taken to the drycleaner, regardless of their label.

❑ Know how to buy clothing that requires little expensive care but still looks good and doesn't wrinkle much.

❑ Know how to judge clothing based on cut, fabric, fit, and

value instead of designer name. Enjoy the way you look, not the way your label looks.

❑ Be able to identify the most common clothing fabrics by sight and feel so you can learn what you like.

❑ Be able to wash, dry, and iron your washable clothes without taking too much time or ruining anything, including using whitener, spot remover, fabric softener, spray starch, and other specialty products.

❑ Have hung a washed item outdoors to dry at least once, just so you can experience the fresh smell.

❑ Be able to iron a shirt, regardless of whether you're male or female, and even though you think you'll never need to do it. You will.

❑ Be able to wash delicate or personal items by hand (in the sink) and then iron them, if necessary.

❑ Know how to hang clothes to avoid wrinkles, which will be either labor-saving or cost-saving.

❑ Be able to thread a needle easily and quickly and tie a good knot just as easily and quickly.

❑ Be able to replace a button, close a split seam, baste a fallen hem, and fix a hole in your pocket.

❑ Be able to fix a zipper that has stuck in place (even while you're getting dressed or undressed) without ruining it unnecessarily.

❑ Be able to polish your own shoes, even if you're female, and know how to care for other leather goods, in order to increase their life.

❑ Have learned how to organize your closets from top to bottom, including your shoes and laundry or drycleaning.

❑ Be able to pull up a window shade without watching helplessly as the roller spins at the top.

❑ Be able to pull down a shade and make it stop at the level you want it to stop on the first or second try.

❑ Be able to raise or lower horizontal blinds successfully on the first or second try without either side going askew.

EXTRA CREDIT

Know where socks that "disappear" in
the laundry actually go.

HOME REPAIR

A determined soul will do more with a rusty monkey wrench
than a loafer will accomplish with all the tools in a machine shop.

—Robert Hughes (1938–)
Australian-born art critic, writer

8

Home Repair

IT WOULD BE IDEAL IF, BY AGE EIGHTEEN, YOU WERE TO:

❑ Have replaced the batteries on everything you use, such as games, music players, and clocks.

❑ Know the function of a fuse box, the appearance of a tripped circuit breaker, and how to reset one.

❑ Know how to tell when you're overloading a circuit without waiting for a circuit breaker to trip.

❑ Be able to safely replace a broken lightbulb and a burned-out bulb in an overhead fixture.

❑ Be able to add an aerator to a sink spout and know how to fix a leaky spout or faucet with a washer.

❑ Be able to retrieve an item that has fallen into a sink drain without a garbage disposal.

❑ Know how to unclog a sink via the drain or the trap and be able to use a plunger successfully.

❑ Be able to fiddle with a commode-tank mechanism and make the water stop running.

❑ Know how to turn off the water under a sink or lavatory in the event of an overflow problem.

❑ Know the location of the main water valve to your home and know how to turn it off, if necessary.

❑ Know about "hard" water and "soft" water and the affect they have on your household environment.

❑ Know the location of your hot-water heater and how it works to supply hot water throughout your home or to your apartment.

❑ Know how and why water pipes can freeze or burst in cold weather.

❑ Know how to clean and change the filters in a furnace (if you live in a house) and an air-conditioning unit.

❑ Be able to clear the drain of a window or wall air-conditioning unit that has been leaking.

❑ Know about insulating a home or apartment in order to reduce cooling and heating costs and be able to handle simple measures, such as installing weatherstripping.

❑ Know why furnaces, air conditioners, and clothing dryers must be vented to the outside.

❏ Know how to test any smoke and carbon-monoxide detectors you may have in your home or apartment.

❏ Be able to detect the odor of natural gas (meaning: the added mercaptan) when you smell it.

❏ Be able to open a window that has stuck shut and to lubricate one that doesn't slide well.

❏ Be able to tighten a loose doorknob before it falls off in your hand and you find yourself stuck inside a room with no other exit.

❏ Know how weather (especially humidity) can affect the movement of doors and windows.

❏ Be able to lubricate squeaky items, such as door hinges, chairs, and dresser drawers.

❏ Be able to open a stuck drawer and to reinsert a drawer that you've pulled out too far.

❏ Be able to attach a simple patch to a window or door screen.

❏ Know what to do if you break a glass object and how to safely clean up the glass afterward.

❏ Be able to mend an object made of glass, china, or pottery. Know what "soldering" means.

❏ Know how to cover scratches in wood surfaces so that you can't detect the damage.

❏ Have watched a few television shows devoted to restoring old homes or repairing problems in newer homes, which can apply to apartments, too.

❏ Be aware of the causes of roof leaks and basement leaks, which will give you a broader awareness of your home environment, especially if you live in a house or may buy one someday.

❏ Know what a septic tank does and what a sump pump does, even if your home doesn't have either one of them. Many homes do.

❏ Know what termites can do and the signs of infestation, even if you live in an apartment.

❏ Be aware of your skill limitations: For example, plumbing is a professional skill, and home repairs are undertaken by the inexperienced at their own peril!

❏ Be aware of your time constraints: for instance, carpentry is a professional skill, too, and you may find it much cheaper to hire a carpenter than to build a project laboriously yourself. Especially if your first effort tumbles down, anyway.

❑ Be aware of your safety obligations: Electrical work (as well as carpentry and plumbing work) is governed by local ordinance (municipal regulation). Many seemingly simple jobs are actually dangerous, both to yourself and to others.

❑ Have watched plumbers, carpenters, and electricians working in your home or apartment—or anywhere else you can learn more about what they do.

❑ Have helped adult members of your household construct temporary solutions for problems that needed handling by professionals until help arrived.

❑ Have helped adult members of your household with home repairs they were able to handle themselves.

❑ Be aware of the importance of household security, know how to tell the difference between various kinds of locks, and be able to assess whether doors and windows are adequately protected.

EXTRA CREDIT

Have used a superglue to mend an object without gluing yourself to the object.

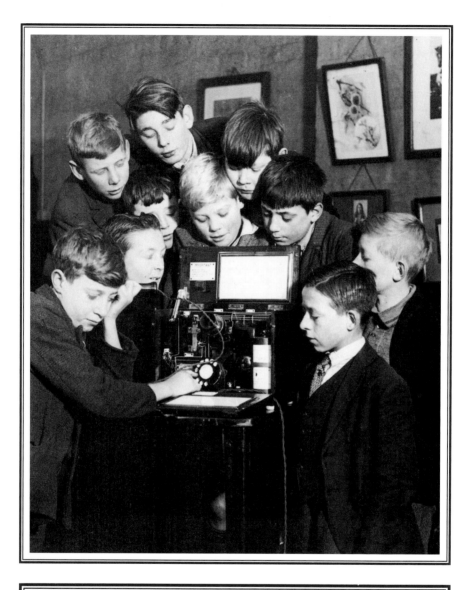

TELEPHONES AND TALKING

Remember that as a teenager you are at the last stage in your life
when you will be happy to hear that the phone is for you.

—Fran Lebowitz (1951–)
American writer

9

Telephones and Talking

IT WOULD BE IDEAL IF, BY AGE EIGHTEEN, YOU WERE TO:

❑ Have strung two cans together and had a conversation with your friend or next-door neighbor.

❑ Be able to call a person your age and chat comfortably for at least a few minutes with his or her parents first, especially if you're calling a member of the opposite sex.

❑ Be able to call your grandparents and chat comfortably for at least fifteen minutes.

❑ Be able to chat comfortably with either one of your parents, regardless of who calls whom.

❑ Be aware of how early and how late you should call people on weekdays, considering factors such as whether the people are family or friends, their ages and habits, and the nature of your message. Also know how weekdays differ from Saturdays, and how Saturdays differ from Sundays.

❑ Be able to sense if you're interrupting the person you're calling and should call back another time.

❑ Be able to diplomatically tell a caller that you cannot take his or her call and would like to talk another time.

❑ Know how to end a call you initiated when the conversation lags or when the other person would like to stop talking.

❑ Know how to gracefully end another person's call without hurting his or her feelings or fabricating anything too silly.

❑ Know how to ask another person to wait for a moment (or put him or her on hold) without causing offense, especially if you intend to take another call.

❑ Be able to telephone someone you don't know, explain who you are, if appropriate, and state your reason for calling.

❑ Be able to modulate your voice so that you can be heard easily during a telephone conversation, but not painfully so.

❑ Be able to answer your home telephone clearly and cheerfully, plus take an accurate message in writing.

❑ Be able to diplomatically handle an incoming call for a member of your family who does not wish to take the call.

❑ Know what to say if you accidentally make a call that turns out to be a wrong number.

❑ Know what to say if you answer a call that you learn is a wrong number and what safety factors must be considered, in case the call was not an accident.

❑ Be able to hang up summarily on telemarketers and other nuisance callers as soon as you recognize the nature of the call.

❑ Be able to leave a concise, complete message on an answering machine or voicemail.

❑ Be able to program the outgoing message on your home answering machine or voicemail.

❑ Be able to operate your home answering machine or voicemail without losing messages and be able to retrieve your messages remotely.

❑ Know how to operate all the buttons on your telephone or answering machine, even if you think you don't have use for them. Once you know how to operate the buttons, you will find use.

❑ Be able to get directory information anywhere in the country to make a long-distance phone call yourself.

❑ Be able to get operator assistance for problems and be able to place a collect call in an emergency.

❏ Know how to use common types of pay phones and calling cards.

❏ Know how a cell phone operates (versus a cordless phone) and how to call a pager.

❏ Have arranged at least one conference call, maybe for family or friends living in other states.

❏ Have navigated automated telephone menus, such as finding flight arrival information about a friend or relative landing soon.

❏ Have looked through all the helpful information in the front pages of the telephone book so you know what is available.

❏ Know how to use the white and yellow pages of the telephone book, plus have at least explored the contents of the "blue pages."

❏ Have examined your family's local and long-distance telephone bills to see how many calls are made, how long they last, and how much they cost, plus the cost of optional services.

❑ Know about all the optional services offered by your local and long-distance telephone service providers and why you need almost none of them.

EXTRA CREDIT

Fully understand the positive and negative aspects of telephone communication. The main advantage is convenience (meaning: you are able to speak with someone who is not present and who may even live or work at a great distance). The disadvantages are serious. When you communicate with someone in writing, you are able to revise your words until your letter says exactly what you wish to say; the drawback is that you cannot see their effect on the recipient. When you communicate with someone in person, the opposite occurs: you cannot revise your words ahead of time, although you can at least see their effect on the recipient. But when you communicate with someone on the telephone, you can neither revise your words ahead of time nor see their effect on the recipient. In short, telephone conversations should be undertaken only in circumstances in which the disadvantages are unimportant.

THE ART OF COMMUNICATION

Most conversations are simply monologues delivered
in the presence of a witness.

—*Margaret Millar (1915–1994)*
American mystery writer

10

The Art of Communication

IT WOULD BE IDEAL IF, BY AGE EIGHTEEN, YOU WERE TO:

❑ Have played the whisper and repeat game ("telephone") to witness how quickly spoken messages change.

❑ Be able to talk with friends and relatives in depth about subjects other than friends and relatives.

❑ Be able to carry on a light conversation for fifteen minutes with a person you don't know at all.

❑ Be able to talk without saying "I" or "my" and without questioning people about themselves.

❑ Be able to give a straightforward one-minute answer, if you wish, when asked about yourself.

❑ Be able to diplomatically decline to answer any kind of question that you don't wish to answer.

❑ Be able to speak clearly and loudly enough so that you are heard by your intended listener and few others.

❑ Be able to tell a joke well enough so that most people get it and maybe even laugh.

❑ Know when to speak, when to listen, and how to gently interrupt as an aid to conversation.

❑ Be able to change the subject when appropriate and comfortably accept another person doing so.

❑ Know which topics are considered taboo, which questions are impertinent, and why.

❑ Know how to praise the ideas of another person for a reason other than simple agreement. Otherwise, you're just praising yourself.

❑ Know how to accept praise for your ideas without seeming to congratulate the other person for agreeing with you.

❑ Be able to accept criticism for your ideas without being defensive, unless you need to explain points that were misunderstood.

❑ Be able to reply diplomatically when challenged incorrectly or foolishly.

❑ Be able to listen to beliefs and opinions that contradict your own without interrupting. You may learn that your own beliefs are incorrect or that your own opinion is foolish.

❏ Know how to criticize the ideas of another person by explaining the reasons for your disagreement. Otherwise, you're just expressing an empty opinion.

❏ Understand the importance of eye contact and facial expression, plus the impact of silence.

❏ Know how body language—including your own—can express both thoughts and feelings.

❏ Be able to use humor to lighten an embarrassing situation or defuse an argument with no potential for positive consequences.

❏ Know how to politely end a conversation you no longer wish to continue.

❏ Be able to admit you are wrong before anyone else knows it, and even if they will never know it.

❏ Know how to apologize sincerely when appropriate, and at least politely when sincerity is impossible.

❏ Be able to advocate for yourself without appearing—or being—selfish or unconcerned about others.

❏ Be able to advocate for someone other than yourself or for a cause larger than yourself.

❏ Have participated in debates in which you argued in favor of positions with which you disagreed.

❏ Be able to keep a secret or promise when you know in your heart that it is the right thing to do.

❏ Be able to say "no" appropriately to a friend, acquaintance, or stranger and stick to it, regardless of pressure.

❏ Be able to read aloud from newspapers, magazines, or books without hesitating or stumbling.

❏ Be able to speak to a small audience of acquaintances or strangers for ten minutes without notes.

❏ Be able to talk with people of differing intelligence without feeling either intimidated or superior.

❏ Be able to communicate socially with people of differing ages, both younger and much older.

❏ Be comfortable socially with people from differing economic contexts, ethnic groups, and religious beliefs.

❏ Be able to handwrite and print legibly enough so that anyone can read what you write.

❏ Be able to correctly spell the words you would like to write and have excellent written grammar.

❑ Be able to correctly pronounce the words you would like to speak and have excellent spoken grammar.

❑ Be able to write a short business letter that conveys information in a clear and logical way.

❑ Be able to handwrite an old-fashioned postal letter to a relative or friend who lives far away.

❑ Know the right way to address an envelope and how much postage to apply, plus how to wrap a package for mailing.

❑ Know the official post office abbreviations for all fifty states without consulting a list.

❑ Have your own personal e-mail account and use it for most of your written correspondence.

EXTRA CREDIT

Have visited the biggest post office in town and asked for a look behind the scenes. This might stop you from ever complaining again about your mail service.

DATING AND DINING

Darling: the popular form of address used in speaking to a person of the opposite sex whose name you cannot at the moment recall.

—Oliver Herford (1864–1935)
English-born American writer, humorist

11

Dating and Dining

IT WOULD BE IDEAL IF, BY AGE EIGHTEEN, YOU WERE TO:

❑ Have asked each of your parents and grandparents about their dating experiences.

❑ Have tried using a funny pick-up line at least a few times, just to see the range of reactions.

❑ Have gone on a "blind date" a few times, if only for the experience, so that you don't wreck your first date with someone you really like.

❑ Have enough nerve to ask anyone appropriate for a date, including those you think probably won't accept.

❑ Be able to decline a date so gracefully that the person isn't embarrassed that he or she asked.

❑ Know at least a dozen different ways to go on a date inexpensively, including having dinner.

❑ Be able to act happy when you learn that your date's little brother or sister will be tagging along.

❏ Be able to afford wherever you take your date and anyone else whom you host for an evening.

❏ Be able to suffer wearing a necktie (boys) or slightly high heels (girls) for an entire evening without complaint or early removal.

❏ Know how to dress up without overdoing it so much that you feel (and look) awkward for the entire evening.

❏ Be able to introduce yourself to your date's family and converse with them for a few minutes without feeling (and looking) lame.

❏ Be able to hold a coat or jacket open without fanfare so that a woman can slip into it easily.

❏ Know how to offer a woman your arm casually or how to take a man's arm gracefully.

❏ Be able to get into and out of a car without struggling or shocking yourself in the process.

❏ Be able to open a door for your date (or assist with a chair) in such a way that you look manly and not magnanimous.

❏ Be able to hold hands with a date in a friendly way, as a gesture of warmth and good cheer, rather than intimacy.

❑ Be able to avoid using cigarettes, alcohol, and drugs as alternatives to being an interesting person.

❑ Be able to dance just one current step well enough to have fun at parties and not just watch.

❑ Learn at least two classic ballroom dances, at least one of them Latin. This will be socially invaluable someday, and the earlier you start to learn, the better.

❑ Know the reasons for all of the taboos of social dining so well that you even avoid them in private.

❑ Know how to behave at a buffet. For example, you take a clean plate for a second helping.

❑ Have learned the difference between a fancy restaurant and a fine restaurant.

❑ Know how to behave at a fine restaurant, which is a telltale measure of social maturity.

❑ Be able to tell which seat is the best one at the table so you can give it to the person you are hosting.

❑ Be able to order dinner while on a date without feeling that you need to include any type of alcohol.

❑ Be able to discreetly summon a waiter and return food that isn't prepared well or that you dislike intensely.

❑ Know how to respond if someone makes the mistake of addressing you when your mouth is full.

❑ Be able to pace your dining to the pace of others so that they don't feel either rushed to finish or prevented from starting the next course because you're still talking while holding onto your fork.

❑ Know how to excuse yourself from the table temporarily, which should not occur either before or during the dinner service.

❑ Know how and how much to tip people who expect gratuities, even in the case of poor service.

❑ Be able to laugh at your mistakes. This helps everyone recover from an awkward moment.

❑ Be able to respect any curfew. Remember: they are just signs of parental love and interest.

❑ Be able to be diplomatic toward your date even if he or she turns out to be less than a dud.

❑ Be able to dodge a kiss so artfully that your date thinks his only problem is his aim.

❑ Be able to resist the temptation to be too intimate too soon. You'll never regret waiting.

❑ Be able to remain unruffled around overprotective parents, especially the kind who do things like turning on the front porch light unexpectedly.

❑ Be able to thank your date sincerely, being neither too casual nor too profuse with false praise.

❑ Have learned how to end a dating relationship so gently that the other person hardly knows it.

❑ Have learned how to accept the end of a dating relationship like a good sport.

❑ Be able to relate your dating experiences to at least one parent or grandparent of the same sex.

EXTRA CREDIT

Have gone to school dances throughout elementary
school and high school, even if you don't dance,
you don't like anybody who goes there anyway,
and besides, you have far better things to do
with your time.

ETIQUETTE AND NICE THINGS TO KNOW

Politeness is the art of choosing among your thoughts.

—*Anne-Louise-Germaine de Staël (1766–1817)*
French-Swiss woman of letters, novelist

12

Etiquette and Nice Things
To Know

IT WOULD BE IDEAL IF, BY AGE EIGHTEEN, YOU WERE TO:

❑ Be able to hiccup silently, or at least without alerting neighbors to your situation. The first hiccup is an exception.

❑ Be able to sneeze without sounding ridiculous. That means neither stifling yourself nor spraying your immediate vicinity.

❑ Be able to suppress a yawn without trembling lips and nostrils, and if you cannot, at least be able to remember to cover your mouth.

❑ Be able to stanch a sniffle without either honking like a goose or ruining the appetite of everyone who can see you. Hint: try blowing your nose (the way you usually do) in front of a mirror and observing yourself objectively.

❑ Be able to stop coughing when it's necessary, such as

when you're at a theater or a concert or in the middle of an important phone call.

❏ Be able to postpone scratching an itch, no matter where it is—even on your nose.

❏ Be able to tie your necktie (boys) or pin your brooch straight (girls) when facing a mirror.

❏ Be able to arrive anytime, anywhere, no matter what—and call if you are unavoidably delayed.

❏ Be able to wait patiently anytime, anywhere. Hint: either exercise (if you're at home) or use relaxation techniques (if you're in public).

❏ Be able to shake hands in a friendly way without squeezing too hard or being limp.

❏ Be able to walk quickly, yet courteously, on a busy sidewalk or in a crowded hallway.

❏ Know when and how to offer someone your chair or seat so that you don't offend a person who doesn't consider himself elderly or disabled.

❏ Be comfortable rising to meet and greet friends and relatives, then taking your seat again.

❏ Know how to introduce people to each other, including offering some information about them.

❏ Know how to address married women who have kept their own surnames.

❏ Know when to use a person's first name and how to address social superiors, such as your elders.

❏ Be able to accept a compliment without simply returning it or saying anything self-denigrating.

❏ Know when to pay the check yourself and when to allow someone else to pay the check.

❏ Know how to pay the check yourself and how to allow someone else to pay the check.

❏ Be able to sit throughout an evening with comfort, even if you're normally an active person.

❏ Be able to control an urge to tap your foot or wiggle something when you're forced to wait.

❏ Be able to tolerate an evening of boredom without complaint, especially when with relatives.

❏ Be able to spend an evening in a room that is too warm or too cool without complaint.

❏ Be able to spend an evening in the company of a person of your own sex who is more intelligent or more attractive or more successful than you without becoming jealous enough to make a negative comment about him or her.

❏ Know how to leave a party, especially if you leave before your host wants anyone to leave.

❏ Know when to go home, which should be slightly earlier than when your host wants you to go home.

❏ Be able to present a bouquet of flowers to someone as naturally as if you do it every day.

❏ Be able to select a gift appropriate for the person, the occasion, and the size of your budget.

❏ Be able to wrap a gift well, considering the price of paper and ribbon a part of the present.

❏ Be able to open a gift and either express your pleasure sincerely or hide your dismay.

❏ Be able to arrange a bouquet of flowers in a vase so well that you're proud of yourself.

❏ Be able to write a thank-you note that is not perfunctory, impersonal, or vague.

❏ Be able to express your congratulations warmly and without a tinge of jealousy or envy.

❏ Know the meaning of RSVP and "regrets only" and respond accordingly—always.

❏ Be able to host a small party for a friend or relative on a special occasion in a creative, inexpensive way.

❏ Be able to host an informal gathering at home, including offering real food that you make yourself and not just opening bags of snacks.

❏ Be able to host a friend or relative for the night, including providing for his or her personal needs.

❏ Know how to be the perfect houseguest, including at the homes of older relatives, such as your grandparents.

❏ Be able to go out with your parents and behave the same way you do with other adults, such as not expecting special attention and not becoming embarrassed at everything they do and say.

❏ Be able to go out with your grandparents and treat them as though they were royalty, even if they usually treat *you* that way at home.

EXTRA CREDIT

Be able to postpone crying, even when it's tough.
That's one difference between kids and adults.

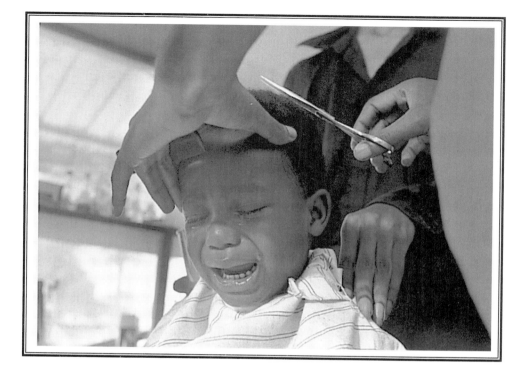

KEEPING CLEAN, NEAT, AND HEALTHY

I've been on a diet for two weeks and all I've lost is two weeks.

—Totie Fields (1930–1978)
American comedienne

13

Keeping Clean, Neat, and Healthy

IT WOULD BE IDEAL IF, BY AGE EIGHTEEN, YOU WERE TO:

❑ Be able to give yourself a good manicure, which has nothing to do with nail polish for women.

❑ Be able to brush and floss your teeth effectively and know how to care for any braces you wear.

❑ Be able to fix your own eyeglasses and know how to care for any contact lenses you wear.

❑ Know how much you should weigh, considering your height, overall frame type, and sex. Note: don't add slightly to your height and frame type, and don't focus on the top of the range.

❑ Have posted your ideal weight on the inside of your medicine cabinet, where you see it daily.

❑ Know how many calories you need to maintain your ideal weight, considering your activity level.

❑ Know how many calories you are actually consuming and strive for the ideal number, instead.

❑ Be in the habit of weighing yourself once a week and writing down the number on a chart.

❑ Know the difference between a balanced diet for your ideal weight and a balanced diet that causes weight loss.

❑ Know what kinds of food you should eat every day—and especially *why* you should—even if you don't.

❑ Know what vitamins and minerals do for you and how their absence can affect your health.

❑ Have recorded everything you eat and drink for a couple of weeks and reviewed the results with a diet professional to see how far you are from a healthy diet that will help you retain your youthful physique or figure for life.

❑ Be in the habit of constantly varying your daily diet, not sticking with your favorites, routinely including foods you dislike (so far), and refusing very few foods entirely. Personal note: I draw my own line at garlic.

❑ Be in the habit of drinking plenty of water each day, especially at meals, whether you like it or not.

❑ Be in the habit of washing your hands before meals and after using a restroom, especially when you're away from home.

❑ Be in the habit of bathing or showering regularly, including washing your hair often.

❑ Know how to get into and out of a bathtub or shower stall safely, no matter what your age.

❑ Have found a simple classic hairstyle that flatters you and that doesn't require special (time-consuming) effort, such as curling or back-combing, which can be saved for special occasions.

❑ Be able to part your hair straight and have found products that keep it under control. Granted, the latter may be impossible, but you shouldn't give up until you're at least 21 years old.

❑ Be able to recognize when you need a haircut and know where to get one inexpensively.

❑ Be able to wash your hair effectively so that it becomes clean but neither too dry nor too oily.

❑ Be able to wash and care for your facial skin effectively so that you don't encourage blemishes.

❑ Know how to prevent premature aging of your skin from exposure to the sun and sunlamps.

❑ Know how to remove stubborn materials (such as paint and glue) from your skin safely.

❑ Be able to shave without nicking yourself (boys) or apply a bare minimum of makeup (girls).

❑ Know all your sizes from head to toe, including your ring size, your glove size, and others.

❑ Be in the habit of experimenting with your clothing (for flattery, not for style) so that you don't get stuck for life with a self-image developed over the course of grade school and high school.

❑ Have stopped in a department store and tried on a couple of hats designed for looks, not warmth.

❑ Know the difference between a steam bath and a sauna.

❑ Have developed a head-to-toe routine that makes you feel clean and neat, and indulge yourself in it whenever you feel stressed or when you just want to reward yourself after a hard day of study or work.

❑ Be in the habit of using exercise as a relief from mental fatigue, especially if you've been working or studying harder than usual.

❑ Have great posture, regardless of whether you've got a great body. This enhances all looks.

❑ Know how much sleep you really need (not really want) and establish the hours as a habit.

❑ Know a few tricks for falling back asleep after you've been rudely awakened, such as when your cat lands on your chest unexpectedly in the middle of a nighttime chase.

❑ Have such regular sleep habits that you no longer need an alarm clock. Hint: don't artificially darken your bedroom by covering the windows.

❑ Be in the habit of getting up bright and early on the weekends just the way you do on the weekdays. Why waste such precious time in bed?

EXTRA CREDIT

Shave even on the weekends (boys) and
wear no makeup on the weekends (girls).

CURING WHAT AILS YOU

For fast-acting relief, try slowing down.

—Lily Tomlin (1939–)
American comedienne, actress

14

Curing What Ails You

IT WOULD BE IDEAL IF, BY AGE EIGHTEEN, YOU WERE TO:

❑ Be able to safely extract a splinter, clip a hangnail, and remove an eyelash from your eye.

❑ Know how to avoid and treat blisters, bug bites, and sunburns, all of which are largely preventable.

❑ Know how to treat minor bruises, scrapes, cuts, and burns and when to get professional help, instead.

❑ Be able to remove a bandage from any part of your body without squealing, at least not audibly.

❑ Know when to use cold packs to treat injuries (usually earlier) and when to use heating pads to treat pain (usually later). Check with your doctor for general rules and specific treatments.

❑ Know how to safely prevent swelling with cold packs, use a heating pad without risking burns, and stop a nosebleed that isn't severe.

❑ Know how to treat minor food poisoning and what symptoms you should take to an emergency room, instead.

❑ Know how to treat a minor cold or sore throat yourself and when to see a health professional.

❑ Know how to treat routine stomach problems, such as what Americans love to call "indigestion."

❑ Know plenty of different ways to treat an ordinary headache, including everything from taking an analgesic to taking a long, brisk walk, plus various combinations of treatments.

❑ Maintain a personal medicine cabinet stocked with everything you need to take care of yourself, including both prescription drugs and over-the-counter medications. Note: Humidity causes many medications to deteriorate. If you take steamy showers, store your medication elsewhere.

❑ Be able to be sick with a minor illness and take care of yourself alone without the need for someone to keep you company and bring you every little thing, like more facial tissues.

❑ Be able to swallow a large pill or give yourself eyedrops without making a big deal out of it.

❑ Be able to drink bad-tasting liquid medication without making all sorts of faces afterward.

❑ Be able to shake down a mercury thermometer in case a digital version isn't handy.

❑ Know what to do to make yourself more comfortable when you have a fever or chills, after checking with your doctor.

❑ Know how to prevent spreading your illnesses to others, including family members, and how to avoid catching contagious diseases.

❑ Know the signs of allergic reactions and have adequate first-aid medication available, even if you seem to have no allergies at present.

❑ Know the signs of anxiety and depression and how to recognize these signs in family members and friends, especially those who may be hiding their symptoms.

❑ Know what diseases and disabilities result from behavioral excess like eating and drinking too much.

❑ Have maintained a detailed, written record (plus a backup copy) of your immunizations and booster shots that you keep throughout life.

❑ Know how to get emergency care, both in your community and when you're traveling.

❑ Know how to gain access to a regular health-care provider if you cannot afford one and do not have insurance.

❑ Know how to find a private doctor and dentist in your community and when to change to another one if the first one isn't suitable for your needs. (Example: he or she is difficult to reach when you're ill.)

❑ Visit your health-care providers for regular checkups, regardless of how healthy you are (or at least how healthy you *think* you are).

❑ Have a record of the information you'll need (both health and insurance information) to fill out a questionnaire at a doctor's or dentist's office before you visit for the first time.

❑ Be able to pay attention to your body and learn to sense when something might be going wrong. Contrast this behavior with people who learn to *ignore* their bodies.

❑ Be in the habit of keeping illness and incident notes for your next visit to a health-care provider and know how to take good notes while you're there.

❑ Be able to read a family medical guide to learn about a specific illness without becoming convinced that you have half a dozen other ones, too.

❑ Be able to discuss bodily functions as well as emotional

problems, even if you're uncomfortable at the time. You'll be way more uncomfortable later if symptoms are neglected.

❑ Be able to admit any fears (such as a fear of needles or the sight of blood) to your health-care provider before undergoing procedures. He or she might know ways to help decrease your discomfort.

❑ Know what to do if you feel faint or dizzy, especially if you might fall and hit your head.

❑ Have enough nerve to ask your doctor if you might need a specialist for a chronic problem.

❑ Understand your health-insurance benefits and know how to use them to get the help you need.

❑ Be in the habit of taking every opportunity to reduce the stress in your life, especially by exercising more.

❑ Have had a whole-body massage by a therapist (or family member) or a neck-and-shoulders massage by a friend.

EXTRA CREDIT

Be able to endure injections, tests, and other medical procedures with patience, dignity, and courage, even when they are embarrassing, invasive, or painful.

EXERCISE AND THE SPORTING LIFE

The first time I see a jogger smiling, I'll consider it.

—Joan Rivers (1933–)
American comedienne

15

Exercise and the Sporting Life

IT WOULD BE IDEAL IF, BY AGE EIGHTEEN, YOU WERE TO:

❑ Have successfully walked across a balance beam many times, without aid and without falling off even once.

❑ Have pretended that you were on the observation-deck railing of the Empire State Building when you were walking across the balance beam.

❑ Have turned cartwheels when you were a kid, even if you gave it up later, when you became too tall to clear the furniture in the living room.

❑ Have engaged in an arm-wrestling contest with a male sibling or relative near your own age. If you're a male, this will be a real contest; if you're a female, be prepared for him to let you win the first couple of times (just for fun . . . and to make sure your arm gets tired) and then suddenly slam your arm back down on the table the next time. That's when you're supposed to give up and admire his amazing strength.

❑ Have engaged in a thumb-wrestling contest with a male sibling or relative who is younger than you. If you're a female, this could be humbling. If you're a male, this could be even more humbling.

❑ Be strong enough to handle your own luggage alone and rearrange the furniture in your room with a teensy bit of help.

❑ Know how to lift heavy items safely, how to set them back down safely (which is of equal importance), and the limits of your strength and fitness.

❑ Have participated in an egg-and-spoon race, a potato-sack race, and a three-legged race.

❑ Maintain a cardiac-fitness regimen that you can continue either indoors or outdoors, depending on the weather.

❑ Maintain an exercise routine for retaining or increasing strength, whether you're male or female.

❑ Maintain an exercise routine just for limbering, regardless of whether you're male or female.

❑ Have signed up for a fitness class to see if the group discipline helps to keep you motivated.

❑ Have arranged to work out with a fitness buddy to see if the mutual peer pressure helps to keep you both motivated.

❑ Be able to do some pushups, situps, and pullups the right way (not the easy way), even if this means you do only a few at first.

❑ Be able to jog for a mile without getting winded and walk for five miles without getting sore the next day.

❑ Be able to swim half a mile, tread water, and float. Also, be able to hold your breath for a minute.

❑ Be able to throw and catch outdoor sports balls of all sizes without breaking your fingers.

❑ Be able to kick outdoor sports balls of all sizes without displacing chunks of sod in the process or humiliating yourself by missing the ball entirely.

❑ Be able to hit a ball with a bat, a tennis racket, or a golf club, even if it doesn't fly quite in the direction you intended.

❑ Have tried really hard to learn how to juggle, which at least is a good lesson in humility.

❑ Have tried to throw a boomerang correctly. With success, it's a good lesson in humility for your dog.

❑ Be able to dribble a basketball, even if you're hopeless at making a basket without the help of a ladder (and a chute).

❑ Be able to bowl without damaging the lane (or your toes) and know how to keep score without help or making "errors" that always seem to be in your favor.

❑ Have attended a major-league sporting event, worn a silly hat, had a hot dog and cold soda, and yelled along with everyone else, even if you didn't know what was going on. (You won't be alone.)

❑ Have learned the rules of your favorite major-league sport well enough to enjoy a good game. (Plus, you'll be able to lead the yelling yourself.)

❑ Be able to play an outdoor team sport yourself, one that you can continue as an adult.

❑ Be able to street skate or ice-skate well enough to remain upright at a local rink, even if you're not all that steady.

❑ Be able to ride a boys' bike with complete confidence, even if you're a girl. (Girls: Boys' bikes are safer and stronger, and how often are you going to want to wear a skirt when you go bike-riding, anyway?)

❑ Have gotten a kite up in the air, kept it there for a while, and managed to bring it back down in one piece, even if it sustained a bit of battering in the process.

❏ Have adopted a solo life sport—meaning, one you can do on your own—such as archery or riding.

❏ Have watched every Olympic sporting event at least once—even the ones in which you thought you were not interested—including both the summer and winter games.

❏ Have tried a self-defense discipline, just to see if you like it and could become an expert.

❏ Have tried a relaxing discipline for the mind, body, and spirit. Yoga is just one example.

EXTRA CREDIT

Have attended a sporting event for children
and cheered for both teams.

ENJOYING THE GREAT OUTDOORS

It's a sure sign of summer if the chair gets up when you do.

—Walter Winchell (1897–1972)
American journalist and radio broadcaster

16

Enjoying the Great Outdoors

IT WOULD BE IDEAL IF, BY AGE EIGHTEEN, YOU WERE TO:

❑ Have caught fireflies on a warm summer evening and watched them glow in your cupped hands.

❑ Have changed to old clothes, gone outside during a summer storm without an umbrella, tried to catch raindrops in your mouth as they were falling, let the water pour down onto your face, and splashed in puddles until you were completely soaked.

❑ Have gone fishing for the first time with your grandfather and used a bamboo (cane) pole.

❑ Have explored streams in search of fabulous gems and woodland wildlife, such as lizards, turtles, rabbits, beavers, turkeys, pheasants, owls, and deer.

❑ Have used binoculars to enjoy wild creatures, such as porcupines, from a safe distance and without disturbing them.

❑ Be able to recognize a few local wild birds and their songs, plus tried in vain to imitate them.

❑ Be able to recognize the dangerous snakes, spiders, insects, and plants that live in your area of the country.

❑ Be able to bait a hook, catch a fish, reel it in, remove the hook, and then clean and cook the fish for dinner that same day.

❑ Be able to hike with friends all day without getting lost, bitten, scratched, or covered with rash.

❑ Have used a compass to keep track of your location while on a hike, even though you and your friends knew perfectly well where you were. (Or thought you did.)

❑ Be able to plan, purchase supplies, and manage a weekend camping trip with family or friends.

❑ Be able to recognize enough kinds of clouds to help you predict the weather for the day.

❑ Have built a campfire with others and cooked a dinner that was not prepared beforehand.

❑ Have toasted marshmallows around a campfire and sung songs with a group or told the kind of stories that you make up as you go along.

❑ Have learned to use maximum care to extinguish a fire

completely, following all forest-service guidelines and instructions.

❏ Have tried making your own soap from bacon fat and wood ashes, even if you made yourself look worse afterward instead of better.

❏ Have pitched your own tent (or helped to pitch a tent meant for more than one person) and spent the night there in a sleeping bag.

❏ Have tried counting the stars on a warm summer night when you're out in the country.

❏ Have watched a meteor shower or any other celestial event that was publicized in advance.

❏ Be able to recognize many of the major constellations and know the stories behind them.

❏ Have looked at the full moon through a telescope, just to appreciate its beauty.

❏ Have sat by a window and watched a fierce lightning storm raging in the distance.

❏ Have gotten up early to go to a special vantage point and watch the sun rise with your grandparents.

❏ Have gone on an automobile trip with your family to see the changing fall colors of the trees.

❑ Have gone apple-picking at an orchard and tried bobbing for apples afterward with your friends.

❑ Have chosen a pumpkin at a farm and helped make your family's jack-o'-lantern afterward.

❑ Have built a snowman at least once, even if you only see snow while driving through the mountains or on vacation now and then.

❑ Have hiked up a mountain at least part of the way, then stopped for a picnic lunch to enjoy the view from the greatest height you could manage.

❑ Have gone sledding in a park or on an open slope, even if your sled was just a big sheet of heavy cardboard.

❑ Have gone on a hayride in the spring, either with a group of people your age or on a date.

❑ Have visited a seashore, where you took off your shoes and walked in the sand and surf.

❑ Have made sandcastles and sand angels, even if you regretted the latter after learning how many showers it takes to feel unsandy again.

❑ Have gathered seashells, gone snorkeling, and tried to grab little fish with your bare hands.

❑ Have helped to row a boat and at least ridden on a sailboat, even if you were useless there.

❑ Have gone swimming with your family somewhere other than a public or private pool.

❑ Have visited a desert and marveled at the animals and plants that thrive in such a harsh environment.

❑ Have explored a tiny part of the fascinating world beneath us by taking tours of famous caves.

❑ Have searched for arrowheads and fossils and any other remnant of the near or distant past, even if you never, ever found anything.

❑ Have gone somewhere wooded on an overcast fall day, especially when a winter storm might be brewing, and listened to the wind.

EXTRA CREDIT

Have seen a gorgeous rainbow and tried hard to memorize the scene forever, returning to it now and then. For example, return to your rainbow and climb it when you have trouble falling asleep.

PLANTS AND TREES

A weed is a plant whose virtues have not yet been discovered.

—*Ralph Waldo Emerson (1803–1882)*
American philosopher, poet, essayist

17

Plants and Trees

IT WOULD BE IDEAL IF, BY AGE EIGHTEEN, YOU WERE TO:

❏ Have blown dandelion puffs, looked for four-leaf clovers, and made a daisy chain.

❏ Have tried to whistle using a blade of grass and sampled the honey from a beehive (safely).

❏ Have tried climbing a tree under your father's supervision until he yelled at you to stop.

❏ Have grown a potato plant long enough to surprise most people who saw it and disgust the rest of them.

❏ Have waited endlessly for a Venus's flytrap to gobble up an insect and then finally given up and tried tricking it with your finger.

❏ Have tended plants in your room, fertilized them appropriately, and watched them grow (or die).

❏ Have turned houseplants away from a sunny window and then observed how they slowly turned back to face it again.

❑ Be able to recognize and name a few local wildflowers, especially the ones that grow nearby.

❑ Have pressed a few wildflowers into a book of poetry and given it to your grandmother, including a handwritten note inside the front cover.

❑ Have dyed white flowers vivid colors, using food coloring, and then presented your mother with a bouquet of the surprising results.

❑ Have dried a few flowers and made a bouquet to give to your sister or another female relative.

❑ Have visited a floral shop, smelled flowers for as long as they would tolerate your presence, and decided on your favorite scent.

❑ Have studied garden styles enough to tell them apart, starting with English and Japanese gardens.

❑ Have taken a tour of local gardens maintained by area residents, for both admiration and inspiration.

❑ Know which of your favorite flowers will bloom only once and which will bloom again and again.

❑ Have planted and tended a flower garden with several varieties, starting with seeds or bulbs.

❑ Have tasted a salad topped with edible blooms, such as pansies and squash blossoms.

❑ Have spent long, satisfying hours weeding your garden and enhancing its beauty.

❑ Have stuffed a set of your father's old clothes full of dead leaves to create a scarecrow, even if the only thing it ever scared was your mother.

❑ Have planted a vegetable garden, defended it from bunnies, and then cooked what you raised.

❑ Have tried to grow your own salad, fought uselessly with the bunnies, and then given up.

❑ Have read about the variety and number of animal pests (both large and small) that might visit your garden and not been overwhelmed by this information. Have tried not to think about your neighborhood dogs and cats, which likely were not included.

❑ Have raised a tomato plant and then discovered how much better your tomatoes taste than the ones you buy at the grocery store.

❑ Have tried to grow an herb garden and then experimented with the results in cooking.

❑ Have learned about which common food plants have both edible and poisonous varieties, such as berries and mushrooms, but never relied on your own knowledge to tell the difference.

❑ Know how to handle insecticides, weed killers, pesticides, and other poisons safely.

❑ Have mowed a lawn without using a riding mower, even if you couldn't do it all in one day.

❑ Have raked leaves, including jumping in the pile afterward and having to rake them again.

❑ Be able to name all the plants that grow on your property, including the weeds.

❑ Be able to recognize and name all the trees on your block and have examined the difference in their leaves.

❑ Be able to identify the trees that bear nuts in your area and have roasted your own chestnuts (bought from a grocery store) or at least sampled a few from a street vendor.

❑ Be able to identify the various fruit trees in your area when they're in bloom.

❑ Have chosen a fruit tree in your neighborhood or community and visited it regularly throughout the year to see how it changes.

❑ Have watched a television show about how maple syrup is made.

❑ Have tried to tell the age of a tree from the rings on its trunk, even if you failed completely.

❑ Have observed workers while they cut and removed a tree to see what precautions must be taken.

❑ Have watched someone chop firewood from a log, just to appreciate the physical nature of the task.

❑ Have planted a tree, either on your own property or elsewhere, and watched it grow over time.

❑ Have gone on a woodland walk in late autumn, especially when the leaves were beginning to fall in earnest.

❑ Have visited a major botanical garden and spent time experiencing the serene beauty of nature undisturbed.

❑ Have visited a tropical rain forest exhibit and marveled at the fabulous plants that grow in this environment.

EXTRA CREDIT

Have chosen as a birthday gift a tiny bonsai tree that you could carefully water, fertilize, and prune for the rest of your life, as a special memory of childhood.

ANIMALS IN OUR WORLD

The best thing about animals is that they don't talk much.

—*Thornton Wilder (1897–1975)*
American novelist, playwright

18

Animals in Our World

IT WOULD BE IDEAL IF, BY AGE EIGHTEEN, YOU WERE TO:

❏ Have taken a pony ride as a child, even if it was just at an amusement park.

❏ Have ridden a horse as a teenager, at least in a riding rink but preferably outdoors.

❏ Have allowed a horse to eat from your hand and marveled at the softness of its nose.

❏ Have attended both a horse show and a thoroughbred horserace to see animals that are considered beautiful and fast.

❏ Have learned about breeding various animals and know the significance of the term "purebred."

❏ Be able to identify the most common breeds of dogs and cats on sight.

❑ Have attended a dog show and a cat show and witnessed what it takes to be a champion.

❑ Have visited a family farm or ranch, spending a weekend or longer, if possible.

❑ Have gathered eggs without either breaking any of them or scaring the chickens.

❑ Have visited a dairy farm, helped to churn butter, and learned how cheese is made.

❑ Have either milked a cow without annoying her or at least fed the goats if you were squeamish.

❑ Have fed some pigs and marveled at how they behave and what they will eat.

❑ Have watched a sheep being shorn of its wool.

❑ Be able to identify a robin, a cardinal, a blue jay, and a few more birds that you like.

❑ Have built a birdhouse from scratch and hung it in a good location, even if you knew that no self-respecting bird would dream of moving into it.

❑ Have identified the birds that moved into your birdhouse, anyway.

❑ Have built a bird-feeding station in a place where you could observe it from home.

❑ Have tried to "squirrel proof" your bird-feeding station in at least six different ways and then accepted the fact that you'd been outwitted by squirrels.

❑ Know the migration pattern of your local birds, including when they leave and return.

❑ Be able to recognize the difference between a bird and a bat swooping across a field at twilight.

❑ Be able to recognize the sight of an eagle or a hawk soaring gloriously in the sky.

❑ Have visited a duck pond and fed the ducks in the recommended way, if permitted.

❑ Have inquired about how wild animals are protected in your area.

❑ Have spent time watching the gorillas and monkeys at a wildlife preserve during feeding time.

❑ Have visited a petting zoo and touched all of the varieties of animals, including those you disliked.

❑ Have visited a wildlife preserve or zoo as a child, at least once a year.

❑ Have visited a wildlife preserve or zoo as a teenager, both in a group and alone.

❑ Have taken a child to visit a children's zoo and remembered how it felt to be so delighted.

❑ Have visited a butterfly house and resisted the temptation to ever catch a wild butterfly again.

❑ Have sheltered and fed a caterpillar and watched it build a cocoon.

❑ Be able to let some kind of creepy crawling critter travel up and down your arm.

❑ Have handled a reptile without squealing and certainly without flinging it away.

❑ Have attempted to follow an ant (either in an ant farm or on the ground) and then given up.

❑ Have turned over rocks to see what kinds of creatures live under them.

❑ Have watched plenty of wildlife documentaries on television, including the ones about bugs.

❑ Have visited a natural history museum several times at different ages, both with others and alone.

❑ Have visited a major seawater aquarium and spent time watching the fabulous creatures there.

❑ Have raised a frog from an egg and learned firsthand why kids are sometimes called tadpoles.

❑ Be able to tell the difference between a frog and a toad.

❑ Be able to tell the difference between a mouse and a rat.

❑ Be able to tell the difference between a fox and a wolf.

❑ Be able to tell the difference between an alligator and a crocodile.

❑ Be able to tell the difference between a mule and a donkey.

EXTRA CREDIT

Have spied a happy raccoon or opossum dining in your trash can or detected an unhappy skunk within a hundred yards, even if you never saw him.

19

Science All Around Us

IT WOULD BE IDEAL IF, BY AGE EIGHTEEN, YOU WERE TO:

☐ Have made ice cream the old-fashioned way—without a machine—using ice and salt and a crank.

☐ Have grown your own crystals and made your own invisible ink, even if it wasn't quite perfect.

☐ Have had a rock collection and tried to identify them, even if you weren't too successful.

☐ Have created your own rainbow with a glass prism and wowed a small child with the colors.

☐ Have experimented with a gyroscope and thought about the forces of a spinning skater.

☐ Have figured out how to make a sundial that works without using written instructions.

☐ Have built a pinhole camera with a box or a can and taken pictures of your parents with it.

❑ Have built a simple radio that actually works, even if you used a kit complete with instructions.

❑ Have revealed the lines of force around a magnet using iron filings and not made a big mess.

❑ Have annoyed all your family members by trying (once) to shock them with static electricity.

❑ Have built a clock that runs on potatoes for power. Or apples, avocados, bananas, or cucumbers.

❑ Have toured a power plant and learned about how electrical power is produced and supplied to the area in which you live. Have asked about how many potatoes it would take to serve your community.

❑ Have ignited a paper towel with a magnifying glass, under the supervision of an adult.

❑ Have created your own working volcano model with vinegar, baking soda, and food coloring.

❑ Have cleaned up the mess afterward but not before taking a news photo of it for posterity.

❑ Have built your own powerful catapult and launched water balloons (outdoors) with it.

❑ Have figured out how to lift your father with a simple wooden lever and convinced him to let you try it.

❑ Have figured out how to weigh your mother with a huge balance scale in the basement or garage and convinced her to let you try it. Suggestion: calibrate your scale about five pounds too light.

❑ Have constructed your own periscope with mirrors and used it to look over the heads of adults standing in front of you the next time your parents have a party to which you are invited.

❑ Have built a simple hearing device that amplifies sounds, such as through a closed door, based on the principle of a stethoscope.

❑ Have used this device to listen to the party from which you were banished after using your periscope.

❑ Be able to read a barometer and know what the readings mean, especially in predicting weather.

❑ Know where to find the weather forecast in your local newspaper and be in the habit of reading it daily.

❑ Have constructed a device to measure rain or snowfall during a storm and then compared your amount to the amount you heard reported on the radio or television.

❑ Know where to find the sunrise and sunset times in your local newspaper and note how the sky looks at those times (exactly, if possible) at least once.

❑ Have observed the phases of the Moon as they progressed over the course of a month.

❑ Have observed the planet Venus through a telescope and tried to identify other bright objects.

❑ Have tried to find a space station or another satellite visible to the naked eye at night.

❑ Have visited every planetarium and science museum that you could, including the ones located in any areas in which you vacation.

❑ Have entered a science fair every year, even with a project that couldn't possibly win anything.

❑ Have studied the winning projects in the science fairs you entered and tried hard to understand them, asking their exhibitors to explain them to you, if necessary. If they constructed the exhibits themselves (without the help of parents or other accomplices), this should be easy and enjoyable for them. (If not, it won't be either one of those.)

❑ Have read an autobiography (or biography) of a prize-winning scientist whose discoveries were in a field you find interesting.

❑ Have read an autobiography (or biography) of a successful inventor whose ingenuity you admire.

❑ Have read about a major ongoing scientific inquiry, such as why dinosaurs became extinct.

❑ Have read about the tricks that underlie the apparent ability to lie on a bed of nails or walk on hot coals without pain.

❑ Have located your "blind spot" with two dots on paper and considered how this characteristic affects your safety, such as when driving automobiles.

❑ Have used a second mirror to reverse your mirror image so that you could see yourself as others actually see you.

❑ Have pretended that you are Archimedes at bathtime and sunk down into a tub while pondering how you are displacing your volume of water and not your weight. Forget the rest of the story about running through the streets naked, shouting "Eureka!". Archimedes' mother *never* would have tolerated this behavior, and neither would yours.

EXTRA CREDIT

Have created your own cartoon character (like Mickey Mouse) and drawn a book of simple cartoons that could be flipped to produce your own movie (and movie star).

SAFETY IN AN EMERGENCY

The calamity that comes is never the one we had
prepared ourselves for.

—Mark Twain, born Samuel Clemens (1835–1910)
American writer, lecturer, humorist

20

Safety in an Emergency

IT WOULD BE IDEAL IF, BY AGE EIGHTEEN, YOU WERE TO:

❑ Be able to stay calm in an emergency, even if you don't know what to do, and *especially* if you don't know what to do.

❑ Have helped to supply and maintain an emergency first-aid kit—including a manual that you have read cover-to-cover and understand—both at home and in any family cars.

❑ Know the location of both the nearest emergency room and the one that your family doctor can visit.

❑ Know how to make an emergency phone call of any kind, either for yourself or for others, not limiting yourself to the national emergency hotline.

❑ Be in the habit of carrying identification, insurance cards, important phone numbers, and a little cash in your wallet and have written the phone numbers of your local police and fire departments in your address book.

❑ Have tested all the smoke detectors in your home and changed their batteries yourself.

❑ Have participated in a fire drill at home, both during the day and at night.

❑ Be able to exit your house or apartment while blindfolded.

❑ Know how to use your home fire extinguisher and when you shouldn't stop to try.

❑ Know what to do (and what *not* to do) in case of a fire. Simply fleeing is not enough. Example: you should close doors behind you as you exit but leave them unlocked.

❑ Know what to do if your clothing ever catches fire, such as while you're camping.

❑ Be able to remain oriented while inside buildings so that you can more readily find your way back out in an emergency.

❑ Know what to do (and especially what *not* to do) if you ever get stuck in an elevator.

❑ Know what to do in case of a gas leak, an explosion, or an earthquake.

❑ Know what to do in case of a flash flood, a tornado, or other violent windstorm.

❑ Know what to do in case of a prolonged loss of electrical power or other important utility, such as telephone service.

❑ Have witnessed, at least on television, how people prepare their homes for a hurricane or a blizzard.

❑ Have helped to stock and maintain an emergency-living cabinet or closet at home for the whole family.

❑ Have learned about disaster relief in your community before an event is imminent and certainly before one occurs.

❑ Have briefly visited all of the emergency shelters in your vicinity and learned the purpose of each one, so if you need immediate assistance, you'll know exactly where to go.

❑ Know what to do if you get lost in the woods.

❑ Know how to behave if you encounter a wild animal, no matter where you are.

❑ Know the signs that an animal is rabid, remembering that this includes all pets in the neighborhood.

❑ Know how to behave around dogs, especially angry ones, including your own pet.

❑ Know what to do if you get lost in an unfamiliar neighborhood, both as a pedestrian and a motorist.

❑ Know how to behave if you are verbally threatened by a stranger or a group of strangers, both when you're alone and when you're with others.

❑ Know how to behave if you are physically threatened by a stranger or a group of strangers, both when you're alone and when you're with others.

❑ Have taken a class to know when to defend yourself and how to be effective.

❑ Have considered how to behave if you are caught in a violent situation, such as a store robbery.

❑ Have discussed with your parents how to behave if you are threatened with abduction or rape.

❑ Have discussed with your parents how to behave if you are verbally or physically threatened by someone you know.

❑ Know what to do if you ever discover a gun or other dangerous weapon.

❑ Have walked through all the rooms in your home with your parents and considered how to make them as secure from intruders as possible.

❑ Have discussed with your parents what to do if you lost your apartment or house keys.

❑ Have attended a safety-awareness class sponsored by your local police department.

❑ Have read a book about basic first aid for any pets you may own, especially noting the sections about taking precautions to protect yourself.

❑ Have completed a basic first-aid course at a local hospital, fire station, or Red Cross chapter.

❑ Be able to perform cardiopulmonary resuscitation (CPR) and the Heimlich maneuver.

❑ Know when and how to use a tourniquet safely and how to treat burns until you can get help.

❑ Know how to treat frostbite until you can get indoors and how to prevent heat exhaustion.

EXTRA CREDIT

Be able to ask for help without waiting for
proof that you need it.

NAVIGATING IN OUR WORLD

When preparing to travel, lay out all your clothes and all
your money. Then take half the clothes and twice the money.

—Susan Heller (1938–)
American author, journalist

21

Navigating in Our World

IT WOULD BE IDEAL IF, BY AGE EIGHTEEN, YOU WERE TO:

❑ Be able to write a clear set of instructions on how to get to your home from nearby highways.

❑ Be able to draw a compass map that shows how to get to your home from several different directions.

❑ Be able to give oral directions to others that are clear enough so that they make no wrong turns, either to your home or to another location with a route you know well.

❑ Be able to listen to oral directions and get enough information so that you find your destination.

❑ Be able to understand oral directions when you're lost, which is more difficult than when you know your current location.

❑ Be able to read both a bus schedule and a subway map well enough to get around town easily.

❑ Be able to tell which direction is north, south, east, and west, at least when you're outside, but preferably when you're inside, too.

❑ Be able to estimate distance (feet, yards, and miles) and time (minutes and hours) better and better as you get older.

❑ Know where the sun rises and sets in the winter months versus the summer months in your area.

❑ Know which are the six major cities closest to your home (regardless of state) in order of their mileage from your home.

❑ Know the shape and size of your home state, which states border it, plus their shape and size.

❑ Be able to read a road map and know the most relevant conventions for your needs. (Examples: interstate highways with odd numbers run north and south; highways with even numbers run east and west; those that bypass a city have three numbers instead of two.)

❑ Be able to plan a trip by car, including sightseeing along the way and visiting family or friends in other locales.

❑ Be able to understand the symbols on highway signs and be able to read a toll-road ticket.

❏ Be able to read a compass and a road map, and to use a globe to view whole countries side-by-side.

❏ Have created travel files with magazine and newspaper articles and other information about places you'd like to visit.

❏ Be able to estimate the cost of a trip, depending on your transportation and destination, and learn about the various ways in which you can save money and still have a wonderful time.

❏ Know what to do when you leave for a vacation. Examples: stop the newspaper delivery and have the mail held; leave your itinerary and contact phone numbers with someone living nearby.

❏ Know the essential items you need to pack for a weekend trip and a vacation of a week or two.

❏ Be able to pack your own suitcase in such a way that your clothing isn't unnecessarily wrinkled and that other items can withstand rough handling.

❏ Know how to travel from your town to a nearby town without a car, either by bus or by rail.

❏ Be able to read train timetables and find your way around an unfamiliar train station.

❏ Have traveled on a train for a long distance, especially

trips with scenic views along the way.

❏ Be able to read airline flight schedules and find your way around an unfamiliar airport.

❏ Have flown on a commercial airliner, even to a nearby destination, and looked out the window during takeoff, landing, and at least a few more times while in flight.

❏ Know when you should leave home to arrive in time to catch a train or plane and the best thing to do if you're running late or miss your departure entirely.

❏ Know the location of the international dateline on the globe.

❏ Understand time-zone changes well enough to determine how long you'll actually be en route.

❏ Be able to determine the time (and day) in other parts of the world after you learn the number of hours they are distant from your own time zone.

❏ Know what documents you might need to visit a foreign country and where you can obtain them.

❑ Have obtained a passport, even if you don't plan on visiting a foreign country any time soon.

❑ Have planned what to do if you are traveling with family or friends and inadvertently become separated from them, especially between destinations.

❑ Have a basic understanding of how a Global Positioning System (GPS) works.

❑ Understand the concept of navigation by the stars just for the satisfaction of knowing it.

❑ Have traveled to a destination by ferry, riverboat, cruise ship, or ocean liner.

❑ Know the location of "port" and "starboard" and the meaning of "knots."

❑ Have read the personal memoir (not biography) of a famous explorer.

❑ Have read the personal memoir of a modern-day traveler.

EXTRA CREDIT

Be able to travel alone, even to a foreign country, with comfort and enjoy yourself, too.

AUTOMOBILE HANDLING AND CARE

"Automatic" simply means that you can't repair it yourself.

—Frank Capra (1897–1991)
Italian-born American motion-picture director

22

Automobile Handling and Care

IT WOULD BE IDEAL IF, BY AGE EIGHTEEN, YOU WERE TO:

❑ Be able to drive a car that has automatic transmission and power steering with confidence.

❑ Have driven a car with a standard (manual) transmission and one without power steering.

❑ Know the difference between front-wheel, rear-wheel, and four-wheel drive.

❑ Have read the owner's manual for the car you drive from start to finish.

❑ Know what to do if you lock the keys inside a car so you won't have to call your parents.

❑ Be able to pump your own gasoline, unless you don't give a hoot about money—which you do, of course.

❏ Be able to change a flat tire, if this is possible for you—which means most males, at least.

❏ Be able to use battery cables to jump-start a car safely, which both males and females can do.

❏ Know what kind of routine maintenance a car needs and how to keep a record of it.

❏ Understand the braking system of a car and know how to maintain it. Your life depends on it.

❏ Know about tire pressure, wheel alignment, rotating the tires, and when to buy new ones.

❏ Have attended a driver safety course and practice the techniques of defensive driving.

❏ Be able to parallel park a car without bumping anything in either direction and know how to park a car on a hill.

❏ Be able to back up a car for a considerable distance in a straight line and back out of a driveway.

❏ Know how to start a car when the engine has flooded or when the weather is very cold.

❏ Know what to do if a car overheats or other warning signals appear on the dashboard.

❑ Know what to do if your car appears to be stuck in mud or snow.

❑ Know how to drive safely when it's raining or when it's snowing. The two conditions are different.

❑ Know what to do if your car breaks down in the dead of winter and help is not available.

❑ Know what to do if your car breaks down in the middle of a hot, deserted area.

❑ Know what to do if your car breaks down in an unfamiliar part of town and you're afraid.

❑ Know how to drive safely in rural areas, where animals may be just around the corner.

❑ Know the special considerations for driving at night and what to do if you become sleepy.

❑ Know how to wear a seatbelt properly so that you don't increase your chance of injury.

❑ Know how to recover from a skid on a dry road and on a wet road.

❑ Know what to do if a tire blows out or the brakes fail suddenly.

❑ Know what emergency equipment and supplies to keep in your trunk.

❑ Know how to use everything you keep in your trunk. You may not always have help handy.

❑ Know what to do if you get into an accident, including neither accusing nor apologizing.

❑ Know what to do if you witness an accident, especially one that involves injury.

❑ Know a good place to get a car repaired, which may not be the closest to your home.

❑ Know which are the most common automobile repairs and why things go wrong.

❑ Know the components of a car well enough so that you can communicate with the mechanic.

❑ Have sat inside a car going through an automated car wash, just for the fun of it.

❑ Have washed a car by hand, inside and outside, plus waxed and polished it, too.

❑ Have buffed off a few scratches in the paint yourself. Not every nick needs expert attention.

❑ Have visited an auto dealership to learn how much extra money it takes to buy a brand-new car.

❑ Know how to locate a good used car, determine a fair price for it, and actually pay that price.

❑ Be able to drive a car full of talking people and concentrate on your driving and nothing else.

❑ Know how to drive safely in major cities, in the suburbs, and on interstate highways.

❑ Know how to rent a car to your best advantage if you don't own one and are planning a road trip.

❑ Be able to operate the security system of the car you drive so well that you use it almost all of the time yet never set off the alarm inappropriately yourself.

EXTRA CREDIT

Be able to be a passenger in a car and not behave like a "back-seat driver."

— An Amateur Photographer —

23

Home and Office Equipment

IT WOULD BE IDEAL IF, BY AGE EIGHTEEN, YOU WERE TO:

❑ Own a simple, inexpensive camera that you use to photograph anything important to you.

❑ Know how to take a good photograph so you won't be disappointed when it's developed—not to mention waste your money. For example: you can't shoot fireworks with a flash.

❑ Have taken photographs with both color and black-and-white film and learned some of the advantages of each.

❑ Know all the functions on your camera and be able to use them to improve your photos.

❑ Know enough about film speed to be able to choose film wisely, varying it for both your subject and the lighting situation, among other factors.

❑ Be able to ask others to take photos with your camera so

that you can be included often without needing a self-timer, which often produces awkward results.

❏ Know how to test most batteries with an inexpensive device so you don't waste money buying new ones unnecessarily.

❏ Know how to adjust the volume control on every device you own that generates noise.

❏ Have investigated all the functions on your alarm clock and tried them all, even waking to music.

❏ Have investigated all the functions on your television remote control, even if you never use them.

❏ Have investigated all the functions on your videocassette recorder, then decided not to use them.

❏ Have installed and programmed a videocassette recorder, plus learned how to set the clock and the timer.

❏ Have helped install all the components of a stereo system, even if it belonged to someone else.

❏ Have tried recording your own voice, even if you were dismayed with the results.

❏ Have tried recording an event with the best videocamera you could borrow.

❏ Know how to safely change the many different kinds of halogen bulbs in various fixtures.

❏ Know how a thermostat operates and the range of sensible settings for winter and summer.

❏ Know how to raise and lower the kinds of pneumatic chairs that are found in many offices, plus make other adjustments for your body size and comfort level.

❏ Be able to load an office stapler, unjam it when necessary, and use a staple remover easily.

❏ Know how to use scissors without ruining them and when using a box-cutter makes more sense.

❏ Know when you can use liquid coverups and when they'll damage sensitive office equipment.

❏ Know how to read a postal scale and avoid wasting money on excess stamps.

❏ Be able to type well using all your fingers—not just your favorites—in the normal manner without having to look down at the keys constantly.

❏ Be able to use a calculator to perform math functions in addition to simple addition and subtraction.

❏ Know how to replace the paper tape in a calculator.

❑ Be able to use a fax machine and know how to fax a piece of paper without writing down the phone number of the recipient on the back of it (or somewhere else).

❑ Be able to use a copy machine and know how to reduce and enlarge images without having to guess where to place the paper through repeated trials first.

❑ Be able to change the cartridge on a printer, copier, or fax, and know how to clean them safely, damaging neither the equipment nor yourself.

❑ Be able to fix a paper jam in a printer, copier, or fax without damaging the sensitive rollers that grab just one sheet of paper and not two sheets or half a dozen. Hint: Turn off the equipment and read the instruction manual.

❑ Have set up your own computer system without help from anyone except tech support.

❑ Have adjusted your monitor to cause the least strain on your vision and have positioned your keyboard, mouse, and other devices to cause the least strain on the rest of your body.

❑ Have learned to listen to your equipment and be able to

tell which sounds indicate the beginning of problems and which sounds are normal.

❏ Have considered repairing your equipment instead of replacing it.

❏ Have tried buying factory-reconditioned used equipment in order to keep your costs down.

❏ Know when you need new equipment and when you're being lured by advertising.

❏ Know when you need new software and when you're being held back by an unwillingness to tackle the unfamiliar.

❏ Be able to use up-to-date word-processing, spreadsheet, and data-management software.

❏ Be able to use e-mail software, internet search engines, and virus software, and know how to keep virus software current.

❏ Have considered spending a weekend with your family somewhere without electricity, just to see what life was like in the days when nothing rang except churchbells.

EXTRA CREDIT

Be able to hold a laser pointer steady while you're pointing to a subject projected on a screen.

ORGANIZING YOUR LIFE

Americans have more time-saving devices and less time
than any other people in the world.

—Duncan Cladwell (1906–1978)
American writer, educator, philosopher

24

Organizing Your Life

IT WOULD BE IDEAL IF, BY AGE EIGHTEEN, YOU WERE TO:

❏ Be able to get up the first time your alarm rings without using the snooze alarm as an aid to getting up at all.

❏ Have found a convenient place to keep frequently used items, such as your keys, where you will always be able to find them without wasting time.

❏ Have set aside an area for items that you need to remember the next time you leave the house, such as an envelope to mail.

❏ Have decided on a dependable method of leaving messages for others in your household, even if this is just a note on the refrigerator.

❏ Have a list of things you need or want to do soon and another list for items to do later.

❏ Have found a handy way to make notes to yourself throughout the day so you don't forget them later.

❑ Have developed your own written system of keeping track of homework assignments.

❑ Be able to create an outline that will help you handle a large job, breaking it down into a logical order, such as which tasks should be done first, which are the highest priority, and which can be grouped together.

❑ Have made a list of household jobs for which you are responsible so that you see how much (or how little) you do.

❑ Have used a timer to learn just how much time you spend on phone calls with your friends.

❑ Maintain a personal appointment calendar, including both one-time entries (such as doctors' visits and social engagements) and recurring events (such as birthdays and holidays).

❑ Have made a habit of carrying work (not just reading material) to appointments and to other places where you may have to wait uselessly, thumbing through old magazines about celebrities.

❑ Be able to cancel an appointment (such as a dentist appointment) as soon as you know you won't be able to keep it, instead of waiting until the last couple of days.

❑ Be able to turn down any request for a social engagement that you don't really want to keep and be able to keep every single social engagement that you do accept (or make yourself).

❑ Have maintained an address book that you keep current with the names of friends and family, plus doctors, dentists, pharmacists, emergency services, frequently called numbers, and much more.

❑ Have set up and maintained a filing system to keep all of the paperwork in your life in one place.

❑ Have organized your filing system in some logical way, such as topical order, with frequently used folders in the front, or in alphabetical order, or chronological order, or some combination of them.

❑ Have maintained a folder with an official copy of all your important documents, such as your birth certificate, and a photocopy of all the documents that you carry, such as your driver's license.

❑ Possess some sort of photo identification, even if you don't drive.

❑ Know the location of the post office that handles your postal mail and know how to contact the service provider that handles your e-mail.

❑ Have maintained a folder of receipts for the purpose of exchanges, returns, or repairs.

❏ Have created a separate folder of paperwork for each of your pieces of equipment (such as a compact-disk player) that contains any instruction manuals, guarantees, warranties, customer-service phone numbers, and authorized-repair location lists that were included in the box.

❏ Have made a habit of discarding papers that are no longer useful whenever you see them and periodically thinning folders that have become suspiciously fat.

❏ Have made a habit of discarding your junk mail without reading it.

❏ Have made a habit of canceling every subscription to anything you don't have time to read.

❏ Have volunteered to help a friend or family member with "pack-rat" instincts to reduce and reorganize their clutter, which will help you eliminate more of your own, too.

❏ Have organized all your closets from top to bottom, including discarding worn clothing and giving away good clothing that you no longer wear.

❑ Have one place where you keep clothing that needs laundering and another place for drycleaning.

❑ Have organized all your drawers and cabinets so that everything is neat and easy to reach.

❑ Have shelved all your books in a logical way, such as keeping schoolbooks or novels together.

❑ Have organized your music collection in a way that makes sense to you, even if it puzzles everyone else.

❑ Have organized any of your belongings that are stored in other parts of the house or garage, such as sports equipment.

❑ Have packed your own belongings for a night spent with a friend and not forgotten anything.

❑ Have packed your own belongings for a family vacation and not needed to sit on your suitcase.

EXTRA CREDIT

Have participated in a household "spring cleaning,"
in which all the rooms in your house or apartment are
thoroughly cleaned, reorganized, and all kinds
of useless stuff is carted away.

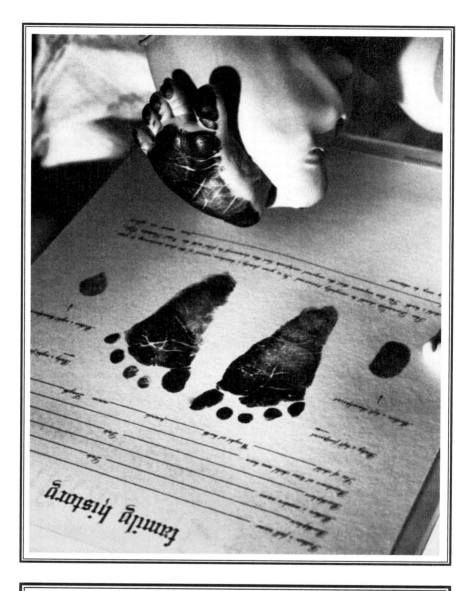

family history

MEDICAL KNOWLEDGE

The art of medicine consists of amusing the patient
while nature cures the disease.

—*Voltaire (1694–1778)*
French philosopher

25

Medical Knowledge

IT WOULD BE IDEAL IF, BY AGE EIGHTEEN, YOU WERE TO:

❑ Have listened to your heartbeat with a stethoscope and have seen an x-ray of your chest.

❑ Have watched an excellent documentary detailing how babies are conceived, carried, and born.

❑ Know the major organs and systems of the body, their general functions, and how they differ between men and women.

❑ Have kept a chronological written record of your own medical history, including such events as serious illnesses, major accidents, surgeries, and allergic reactions, as well as routine vaccinations.

❑ Have developed—with the help of your parents—a brief written record of the medical history of your immediate family members, including your siblings, parents, aunts, uncles, and grandparents.

❑ Have had your hearing and vision checked by a professional and have a copy of any prescription for corrective lenses.

❑ Know your blood type, your cholesterol level, and any routine findings that are abnormal, even if they seem unimportant.

❑ Know how to take your pulse and what the normal range is for people of your age and conditioning.

❑ Know your last blood-pressure reading and the ranges considered desirable and acceptable.

❑ Have seriously considered agreeing to organ donation on the back of your driver's license.

❑ Know the symptoms of the illnesses that often strike people of your age, sex, and ethnicity.

❑ Know the warning signs of major illnesses, such as diabetes, cancer, and heart disease, even if you think you are too young to develop such conditions.

❑ Understand how caffeine affects the human body, what beverages contain it, and in what quantity. Note: chocolate contains caffeine.

❑ Know the alcohol content of beer, wine, and liquor, the different ways they affect different people, how much blood alcohol is too much, and the risks of both addiction and fatal poisoning.

❑ Have seen photographs of healthy pink lungs and the blackened lungs of people who smoke cigarettes. Cigars are a health hazard, too.

❑ Have read, heard, or watched a first-person account (preferably a documentary) of the horrors of drug addiction. This should *not* be a movie, complete with handsome stars who die poignantly.

❑ Have watched a medical documentary about the physical and mental conditions that develop in a person dying of AIDS.

❑ Know the best sources of medical-reference material but only as a supplement to your doctors.

❑ Know your anatomy well enough to be able to describe symptoms accurately to your doctors.

❑ Know the names of the main medical specialties to help you realize when you might need one.

❑ Know about the major medical technologies and most common tests, so you won't be unnerved if you need them. Examples: CAT scans and ultrasound imaging.

❑ Know how anesthesia works, so you'll be less afraid of a surgical procedure if you need one.

❏ Know the difference between bacteria and a virus, and why infections caused by each are treated so differently.

❏ Know the names of any prescriptions you receive, their intended purpose, and how they work.

❏ Know how your favorite over-the-counter remedies—such as pain relievers—work and how to choose the right ones for your needs.

❏ Be able to open all childproof caps without resorting to power tools.

❏ Know which medicines you should never mix together or with other drugs, like alcohol.

❏ Know which vitamins and minerals can cause harm when taken in excess.

❏ Know the difference between FDA-approved medicines and alternative medicines.

❏ Know where you can go for information and support if you have a special condition.

❏ Know the difference between a psychiatrist, a psychologist, and a social worker.

❏ Know what social workers do (and don't do) and how to get their help, if necessary.

❏ Know where to go for free or low-cost services, such as vaccinations and blood-pressure checks.

❏ Know how your health-insurance plan operates so you can get the best possible care available.

❏ Know how aging is affecting your grandparents and your parents, too. One day—if you take good care of yourself and are very lucky—you will be old, too.

EXTRA CREDIT

Have decided whether you want or need birth control and have obtained it ahead of time, preferably with the knowledge of your parents. This is one of the most important actions you will ever take. And although the following statement may be difficult to believe, I personally guarantee that if you do not sleep with anyone before you are married, you will never regret that decision. This counsel has nothing to do with morality. Instead, every other action is a gamble with your future.

26

Consumer and Shopping Skills

IT WOULD BE IDEAL IF, BY AGE EIGHTEEN, YOU WERE TO:

❑ Be able to shop for groceries alone and get good, healthy food value for your money.

❑ Be able to estimate how much food you need to buy so you won't be tempted to eat too much in order to avoid wasting too much.

❑ Be able to read ingredient labels and not be distracted or misled by packaging claims.

❑ Know how to choose the best and freshest fruits, vegetables, meats, and dairy items.

❑ Know the various cuts of meat and why their prices can differ so dramatically.

❑ Know which food you should buy fresh, which you should buy frozen, and why.

❑ Know how the price, quality, and taste of produce varies with the season.

❏ Know why certain foods, such as truffles, are expensive. It's not because they taste best.

❏ Know how to use coupons to save, not to spend more, including not spending too much time clipping and shopping at too many different stores.

❏ Know when to take advantage of sales and when the sales take advantage of you.

❏ Understand unit pricing so you can shop by comparing competing products.

❏ Know a few tricks, such as always using a list and never shopping when you're hungry.

❏ Be able to shop for clothing that won't go out of style before you wear it out, unless you have an unlimited source of funds for this purpose, which you do not. Suggestion: glance in your closet at what you thought was stylish only six months ago.

❏ Have the confidence to go shopping for clothing alone (meaning: without friends) and to ignore the comments of salespeople, who are trained to be polite and will never gasp at the way you look in running shorts.

❏ Be able to tell whether garments that look good on the hanger actually look good on you.

❏ Be able to tell whether a color or pattern is flattering to you or whether you just like it.

❏ Be able to combine colors and patterns in such a way that you don't look just plain nuts.

❏ Know how to choose outerwear that accomplishes its purpose, such as keeping you warm or dry. Remember: you'll be wearing it outdoors, not in a dressing room.

❏ Know how to buy shoes that suit your activities and fit well, instead of shoes that are in style.

❏ Be able to update a wardrobe inexpensively. Example: keep your clothes simple and update only your accessories.

❏ Know how to select jewelry that enhances your appearance instead of subtracting from it.

❏ Be able to go shopping for a bathing suit and not become depressed afterward.

❏ Know the difference between designer merchandise and quality merchandise.

❏ Know when designer names add little besides cost. Examples: sunglasses, jeans, and watches.

❏ Know when quality merchandise adds little besides cost. Examples: ties, scarves, and belts.

❑ Be comfortable returning an item, if possible, to a store for replacement, exchange, store credit, card credit, or cash.

❑ Know how to effectively voice a complaint or make a claim at a retail store.

❑ Be comfortable bargaining for all sorts of purchases. You can practice at garage sales. Suggestion: practice in another neighborhood!

❑ Know how to research major purchases before you actually go shopping for them.

❑ Know how to evaluate competing brands, including noting features (which are always mentioned) and looking for shortcomings or missing features (which are never mentioned).

❑ Be able to evaluate and select your own computer system, including the printer.

❑ Know how to select electronic equipment that meets your needs and does not exceed them.

❑ Understand how extended guarantees and warranties make sense in some cases and not in others.

❏ Know how, when, and where to save money by buying used products, including clothing.

❏ Know how to find the true value of jewelry, gold, silver, coins, stamps, and antiques.

❏ Know how to select a diamond, why you are unlikely to do a good job, and why you don't ever need a diamond for anything, anyway.

❏ Be able to easily decline the offers of salesmen at your door, on the phone, and on the street.

❏ Know how installment plans work and the total cost of any merchandise you buy this way before signing the contract. Also, know about any rights you may have in case you regret your decision afterward.

❏ Know how to find the name of agencies to contact if you believe you're the victim of a fraud.

EXTRA CREDIT

Be familiar with the shopping districts in your city and have explored all the areas that make sense for your budget, instead of constantly returning to the same shops at the nearest mall.

DESIGNING AND BUILDING

Architecture begins when you place two
bricks *carefully* together.

—*Ludwig Mies van der Rohe (1886–1969)*
German-born American architect

27

Designing and Building

IT WOULD BE IDEAL IF, BY AGE EIGHTEEN, YOU WERE TO:

❑ Have assembled "houses" and all sorts of buildings using tabletop construction kits.

❑ Have built at least one makeshift contraption that required the use of many tools.

❑ Have used a carpenter's level all over your apartment or house to learn what's really level and what's really not, including everything from the floor in your room to the kitchen table.

❑ Have visited a hardware store often and become familiar with as many items as possible.

❑ Know which hand tools perform which functions and how to use them around the house.

❑ Know common tool conventions, such as turning right to tighten and turning left to loosen.

❏ Have a tool kit that you know how to use, including smaller items such as nails and washers.

❏ Be able to drive a nail straight into a piece of wood or a wall without smacking your fingers.

❏ Be able to remove nails, staples, and other items securing shipments that have been boxed.

❏ Know how to use knives safely and be able to sharpen them without cutting yourself.

❏ Be able to operate basic power tools, such as a drill, including changing the drill bits.

❏ Know how to use a folding ladder safely, including how high you should ever climb on it.

❏ Be able to assemble furniture (like shelving) from a kit, including replacing the pieces that surely were missing from the box.

❏ Be able to hang a picture straight without making extra holes in the wall or becoming furious.

❏ Be able to paint neatly, including cleaning up the mess afterward and storing the supplies safely.

❏ Have enough sense to know (ahead of time) when your skills will not extend to wallpapering.

❑ Be able to measure accurately for ordering furnishings such as wall treatments and flooring.

❑ Be able to hang a simple curtain rod without feeling humiliated afterward.

❑ Be able to measure for furniture so that it will fit through the front door, around any corners, and into the space you have in mind without deconstruction of any rooms.

❑ Have drawn your room and its contents to scale and then tried rearranging your furniture, if only on paper.

❑ Have taken part in redecorating your room when you became a teenager, considering colors, patterns, and fabrics that were within your family budget.

❑ Have chosen paint from a paint chip and then been shocked by the results of a test patch on the wall.

❑ Have learned how to estimate square footage by using your feet and a little mental math.

❑ Have considered your dream house (within reason) and then tried to draw all the rooms to scale.

❑ Have visited empty lots of known size so you could see a quarter-acre lot, a half-acre lot, and a full-acre lot, even if you intend to live in an apartment.

❑ Have explored the real-estate section of your newspaper a

few times to see how apartment rentals and home prices are affected by their location, lot size, and the living space they offer.

❑ Have closely examined a scale model of a famous building in your town or city.

❑ Have looked at cutaway models of buildings intended for special purposes, such as major museums.

❑ Be able to estimate the number of seats in theaters, concert halls, and stadiums, first by trying to count people and rows, then by just glancing around the room. Note: the box office has this information—just ask.

❑ Be able to read blueprints, floorplans, and other diagrams used in the construction process.

❑ Have visited a single construction site numerous times during the process of building a nearby home or business.

❑ Have watched large equipment (such as cranes) at work during the process of constructing a major building.

❑ Have watched documentaries about the construction of modern skyscrapers, bridges, and dams.

❏ Have watched documentaries about the construction of modern ships and aircraft.

❏ Have watched a documentary about the assembly of the Statue of Liberty.

❏ Have watched documentaries that contain footage filmed during famous construction projects from earlier days, such as the Golden Gate Bridge and Hoover Dam.

❏ Have inquired at your local department of public works about any new roads or highways being built or planned in your vicinity and asked to see any before-and-after contour models they may have constructed.

❏ Have watched construction workers resurface a road, repair potholes, and lay a sidewalk.

❏ Have witnessed buildings being demolished, even if only on television.

EXTRA CREDIT

Have watched an old-fashioned "barn raising" on television.

BUSINESS AND FREE ENTERPRISE

Being in your own business is working eighty hours a week so that you can avoid working forty hours a week for someone else.

—*Ramona E. F. Arnett (1906–)*
American architect, author

28

Business and Free Enterprise

IT WOULD BE IDEAL IF, BY AGE EIGHTEEN, YOU WERE TO:

❑ Have participated in a bake sale and not eaten all your profits by the end of the day.

❑ Have sold cookies or useful household items (not trinkets) for a major nonprofit organization.

❑ Have run a lemonade (or other cool drink) stand and made a profit by the end of the weekend.

❑ Have named your business and created a poster to display in front of your stand, designed to attract customers and not detract from the looks of the neighborhood.

❑ Have hired a younger person, not including relatives, to help you at your stand and paid him or her a wage appropriate to the work performed and not to his or her age.

❑ Have bartered services you like to perform or are good at performing (example: weeding a garden) in exchange for the services of another person (example: cleaning a garage).

❑ Have run a small-service business, such as delivering papers, mowing lawns, or walking dogs.

❑ Have kept simple accounting records for your business to track your income and expenses.

❑ Have tried a special promotion, like "buy two, get one free," and noted whether you sold more goods or services, plus whether your profit increased or decreased.

❑ Have tried raising and lowering your prices and noted whether you sold more goods or services, plus whether your profit increased or decreased.

❑ Have run a business with a friend as a partner and noted whether this arrangement proved beneficial for both of you, just one, or neither.

❑ Have run a nonprofit service business for the older people in your neighborhood—performing services like shopping for groceries, cooking dinner, and cleaning—and charging little more than your expenses.

❑ Have organized or participated in a garage sale (or tag sale) and then donated the remainder of the items to charity, instead of selling them for a fraction of their value to a business that buys such remainders.

❏ Have held a job dealing directly with the public, such as in a coffeehouse or restaurant.

❏ Be able to handle customers effectively, regardless of their temperament or yours.

❏ Have held a job in any kind of retail establishment in which merchandise is sold to the public.

❏ Be able to work in a subordinate capacity without resenting your supervisors or the managers of the establishment.

❏ Have held a job working in an office environment, whether you were paid or not, including internships.

❏ Be able to work for and with others in the office who may or may not be people you would enjoy as friends.

❏ Have developed a list of references from your work experiences, not including any relatives.

❏ Have asked whether you might be able to go to work with your father or mother (or grandfather or grandmother) for a day.

❏ Have spoken with a few successful entrepreneurs and asked what they thought was important to know about starting a business.

❏ Have visited your local Chamber of Commerce and asked

about resources for business-owners.

❏ Have thought about what you love to do and whether you might be able to develop a business based on this love someday.

❏ Have considered the needs of society and whether you might be suited to a life devoted to public service by founding a nonprofit organization.

❏ Have read a biography of a man or woman you admire who founded a major nonprofit organization.

❏ Have read a real-life success story or rags-to-riches biography about a major entrepreneur.

❏ Have read about the subjects of patents, trademarks, servicemarks, and copyrights.

❏ Have watched the stock of a company for whom a relative (or relative of a friend) works and noted the relationship between news about the company and the stock price.

❏ Have pretended to invest one thousand dollars in stocks, then watched the markets to see what happened to the prices of your choices.

❏ Have explored the financial section of the newspaper, just so you could see the various types of information that is important to interested people.

❏ Know the names of the major American labor unions and whom they represent.

❏ Know the most important events in the history of the labor movement in this country.

❏ Know the most important laws that affect workers, such as those pertaining to minimum wages and job safety.

❏ Know what labor issues are current: What do American workers want and need today?

❏ Know what business issues are current: What do American business-owners want and need today?

EXTRA CREDIT

Have donated your services to a fundraiser for
a worthy cause, such as answering pledge telephones
for your local public television station or radio station.

MANAGING YOUR MONEY

The difference between playing the stock market and
the horses is that one of the horses must win.

—Joey Adams (1911–1999)
American comedian, newspaper columnist, actor

29

Managing Your Money

IT WOULD BE IDEAL IF, BY AGE EIGHTEEN, YOU WERE TO:

❑ Have owned a piggy bank as a child and "deposited" your gift money into it routinely.

❑ Have opened a savings account and checking account with the money you've earned working.

❑ Have contributed regularly to your savings account, depositing all your earnings, if possible.

❑ Have written your own checks in payment for any special items that you bought for yourself.

❑ Have made a deposit by postal mail and withdrawn cash at an Automated Teller Machine (ATM).

❑ Know how to check your account balances and transactions at any time, either online or using an automated telephone system.

❑ Have balanced your accounts by hand, even if you bank online, to learn the logic of how the system works.

❑ Know how to purchase and cash a money order, in case of an emergency.

❑ Know how to wire funds and how to receive wired funds, in case of an emergency. Don't wait until the situation occurs, when you might not be able to obtain the necessary information quickly.

❑ Know the difference between various types of financial institutions, such as banks, savings and loan associations, and credit unions.

❑ Have learned how (and how long) to keep, file, and categorize receipts and other documents for income-tax purposes.

❑ Have filed the number of any accounts—plus every personal identification number (PIN)—that you own, including any credit cards.

❑ Know what people keep in a safe-deposit box and have visited one, if possible.

❑ Have taken part in family shopping for everything from food to furniture, in order to learn about prices.

❑ Know how to search for a good apartment that you can afford, preferably paying for it yourself.

❏ Have made a list of free community resources, such as medical care, education, and entertainment.

❏ Know how mortgages and loans work, including the total dollar amount of interest that will be paid over time, plus how much of each repayment reduces the principal amount and how much goes to interest, especially if this changes over the life of the loan. Don't wait for the shock to arrive when you're older.

❏ Have developed—with advice from your parents—a sample budget for an income you expect.

❏ Have developed another sample budget for an income significantly below what you expect.

❏ Know about all your tax obligations—including social security and medicare—and how much they will reduce the income you have available for supporting yourself.

❏ Have looked at the blank tax forms that your parents will prepare, just so you can see the paperwork and information necessary to complete the process.

❏ Know what kinds of insurance (such as health insurance and life insurance) a person needs at different stages of life.

❏ Have become aware of how routine monthly charges for unnecessary goods and services—such as telephone-company voicemail and enhanced television

entertainment—affect your family budget.

❑ Have become aware of how seemingly small charges for unnecessary goods and services—such as nonstandard checks, frequent ATM usage, and overdraft protection—affect your family budget.

❑ Have become aware of how unnecessary penalty charges—such as for paying your bills late—can affect your family budget.

❑ Be able to compare credit-card programs and understand how they can help or hurt you.

❑ Know the difference between a debit card, a charge card, and a credit card.

❑ Have read personal accounts of people who have gotten into serious trouble with credit cards.

❑ Know about credit ratings, how they are compiled, and how they can affect your borrowing power, apart from obtaining credit cards.

❑ Know what happens when an individual declares bankruptcy and how it affects his or her life.

❏ Understand why casinos and racetracks stay in business—the gambler always loses over the long term.

❏ Have discussed with your parents how loaning money to a friend or relative will affect your relationship with that person.

❏ Have made a habit of giving money to worthwhile nonprofit organizations that you plan to continue throughout life.

❏ Have investigated various well-known nonprofits to see how much money goes to the cause they support and how much money goes to support the organization itself.

EXTRA CREDIT

Have spent a Sunday evening with your parents adding up all the money they have spent on you (including 20 percent to 30 percent of housing costs, automobile expenses, family vacations, and so on) since you were born, plus the money they likely will spend in the future, such as for your college education, and asked how you can ever possibly repay them. Then (when you were alone) thought about how much *time* they spent, too.

CRITICAL THINKING SKILLS

A great many open minds should be closed for repairs.

—*Attributed to the Toledo* Blade

30

Critical Thinking Skills

IT WOULD BE IDEAL IF, BY AGE EIGHTEEN, YOU WERE TO:

❑ Be able to follow an instruction manual without complaining that it was poorly written.

❑ Know when you don't really need an instruction manual and can exercise your mind by doing without it.

❑ Be able to set every clock in your house without the instruction manual (after using it the first or second time, if necessary) when moving back and forth from daylight saving time.

❑ Be comfortable trying to find your way without directions or a map, whenever it makes sense.

❑ Be able to take useful notes on any subject, including subjects with which you are unfamiliar, which is much more difficult.

❑ Be able to meet any deadline, even if your work is done

less well than it would be if you had all the time you would have preferred.

❑ Be able to describe anything visual, such as a street scene, in words that convey your meaning.

❑ Be able to read aloud smoothly from any newspaper, magazine, or book printed in your native language.

❑ Be able to speed-read when absolutely necessary and at least get the gist of the information.

❑ Be able to do minor math calculations without a calculator, using a pencil and paper, instead.

❑ Be comfortable thinking in a twenty-four-hour system and barely notice the difference when you see the time displayed that way.

❑ Have tried to become as comfortable with the metric system of measurement as you are with the English system of measurement, starting with your height and weight.

❑ Become proficient at guessing the time of day (without looking at the sky) and the temperature in your immediate environment, indoors or outdoors, regardless of the forecast.

❑ Become proficient at estimating distances (feet and miles) and durations (minutes and hours).

❑ Own an excellent print dictionary—not an abridged version—that you use routinely to improve the precision of your understanding and thinking.

❑ Be a fine speller, which is largely a function of study and effort, not just intelligence.

❑ Own a complete set of reference works, electronic and/or print, that you use routinely.

❑ Be thoroughly familiar with your local public library and know how to access all its resources.

❑ Know what sections are in your daily newspaper and visit them all now and then, just to see what useful information you might be missing.

❑ Be in the habit of reading at least the front page of your local newspaper every day. Reading the front page of more than one newspaper is even better.

❑ Be able to find names, street addresses, e-mail addresses, and phone numbers online.

❑ Be able to tell the difference between information, misinformation, and disinformation online.

❑ Know how to think critically—the intellectual equivalent of driving defensively.

❑ Be able to analyze statistics, which can be used to support or undercut almost any argument.

❑ Be able to defend your arguments in a rational way. Otherwise, all you have is an opinion.

❑ Be able to recognize the difference between prejudice, bias, and an individual point of view.

❑ Be able to recognize when you're reading or hearing material biased to your own side.

❑ Be able to recognize weaknesses in your arguments and acknowledge them to yourself.

❑ Know the difference between deductive and inductive reasoning and when to use each.

❑ Know all the logical fallacies and be able to recognize them when you hear them.

❑ Have studied logic somewhere, somehow: you'll learn *how* to think, not *what* to think.

❑ Be able to meditate on a subject that concerns you, in your spare time or while listening to music.

❑ Know how to use both outside advice and a pro-and-con list to aid in making better decisions.

❑ Understand the complex interplay between thinking and emotion, and how each affects the other.

❑ Watch public television and listen to public radio, instead of commercial channels and stations.

❑ Spend waiting moments doing crossword puzzles or reading a book you brought yourself.

❑ Play thinking games such as "twenty questions" with another person when you have spare time.

❑ Play strategy games like chess or checkers with others (preferably) or with computers.

EXTRA CREDIT

Be able to figure out which long-distance phone company and frequent-flight program is best for you!

PREPARING FOR THE FUTURE

I like work; it fascinates me. I can sit and look at it for hours.

—Jerome K. Jerome (1859–1927)
English novelist, playwright

31

Preparing for the Future

IT WOULD BE IDEAL IF, BY AGE EIGHTEEN, YOU WERE TO:

❑ Have spent at least one weekend at home alone—unaccompanied by friends or anyone else—that included cooking for yourself (not going out), and accomplishing something worthwhile during the time.

❑ Have spent at least a week at the home of a friend (not a relative) when your parents were on vacation or away on business.

❑ Have spent at least two weeks at an overnight camp during the summer, not seeing your family during that time.

❑ Have spent at least a month in the summer with relatives (if possible) or friends in another city or country—the farther away from home, the better.

❑ Have considered a summer internship in another city or becoming an exchange student in another country.

❏ Have finished tasks you disliked without complaint and performed your best, regardless.

❏ Have learned to do something at which you were no good at all—such as drawing a horse or replacing a doorknob.

❏ Have taken an aptitude test designed to assess your abilities and then used the results only to add to your possible areas of interest, not to subtract from them.

❏ Have entered every contest or competition that suited your talents and a few that didn't, just to see how much you could rise to the occasion.

❏ Have considered your goals in life yearly, ranking them in order. (Fame? Fortune? Family?)

❏ Have made a list of possible career choices, including those suggested by your parents.

❏ Have spoken at length with people currently in those careers, especially your own choices.

❏ Have considered your father's or mother's careers, especially if they are successful and can give you a head start. If you are lucky enough to have the opportunity to join a family business, have seriously considered the possibility before college (so you can take courses that will help) and have resolved to further consider it throughout your education and afterward.

❏ Have attended as many career fairs as you could, mainly to see how much you may be missing.

❏ Have explored information published by the Department of Labor to learn about current job trends, such as which fields or careers are growing rapidly.

❏ Have stopped to consider fields that you might initially bypass, such as the military, which offers a life of great honor, dignity, and security, not to mention benefits like enhanced physical fitness, if not high pay.

❏ Have researched the typical starting salaries for employees in the fields in which you are currently interested.

❏ Have considered how much advanced schooling might be required for your career choices.

❏ Have considered where you might need to live in order to pursue your career choices effectively.

❏ Have researched a dozen different companies from the fields in which you are interested.

❏ Have begun to develop your networking skills by starting a file of names (along with identifying information, phone numbers, and so on) of people who might be able to help you someday.

❏ Have practiced doing interviews for employment with a person who has hired employees himself or herself,

excluding relatives or friends.

❑ Have written your first résumé and not included any references who are relatives or friends.

❑ Have written a cover letter and had it critiqued by adults who are employers themselves.

❑ Have tried to get part-time jobs or internships in the workplaces of your career choices, in order to experience the working environment and see what people actually do all day every day.

❑ Have worked for an employer who is not known personally to your family or friends.

❑ Have read all through the help-wanted ads in your local newspaper, including the sections for which you are overqualified and underqualified.

❑ Have visited a few colleges, including at least your local ones, even if you don't want to go to college at all.

❑ Have spoken to recent graduates about their college experiences, especially those who attended colleges in which you are interested.

❑ Have applied as a freshman to at least two colleges, even if you don't want to go to college at all, just to see if you are accepted at one.

❑ Have decided to continue your education beyond high school, preferably to college, but at least in some way, no matter what form this takes.

❑ Have a social security number and know how much and how little it will help you someday.

❑ Be able to live with a roommate, even if you don't want to and think you will never find it necessary.

❑ Be able to live alone, even if you don't want to and think you will never find it necessary.

EXTRA CREDIT

Have written a draft of a life plan after your sixth birthday, focusing on the things you love to do and the accomplishments of people you admire. File the plan in a folder. Without looking back at it, write a new plan each year, focusing on whatever makes sense to you at the time. Don't look back at any of them. Then, before writing the plan for your sixteenth birthday, reread all of your plans in chronological order.

BEING A GOOD CITIZEN

Half of the American people have never read a newspaper. Half never voted for the president. One hopes it is the same half.

—Gore Vidal (1925–)
American novelist, critic, screenwriter

32

Being a Good Citizen

IT WOULD BE IDEAL IF, BY AGE EIGHTEEN, YOU WERE TO:

❑ Have visited polling sites at the time your parents voted.

❑ Know when, where, and how to register to vote, why you should educate yourself about the candidates and the issues before voting, and why voting is so important.

❑ Have volunteered to help disabled or elderly voters get to the polls on Election Day.

❑ Have researched (for yourself, making no assumptions beforehand) the basic principles of all the major political parties, not just the two most popular parties.

❑ Know where to get nonpartisan information on issues and candidates, including their voting histories.

❑ Know the names and political parties of your senators and representatives in Washington.

❑ Know the names and political parties of your state and local representatives.

❑ Know how your representatives stand on major national or state issues and on the issues that are important to you personally.

❑ Know the difference between principles based on right and wrong versus principles based on personal gain, and consider the basis of your own principles.

❑ Know which officials are voted into office and which are appointed, and by whom.

❑ Know how to contact your elected local, state, and federal officials.

❑ Have attended a community or citywide meeting about an important local issue.

❑ Have written an article for your school newspaper once a year, even if it was never published.

❑ Have made a habit of reading both the editorial and op-ed pages of your newspaper, making sure to include all the articles, not just the ones with which you already agree.

❑ Have sent a "letter to the editor" to a magazine or newspaper regarding an issue about which you had something to say that hadn't already been said.

❑ Be able to notice all the confusion between fact and opinion that appears in the news.

❑ Have learned the requirements of running for local office, including the first step to take.

❑ Have worked as a volunteer for the Democrats, especially if you're a Republican.

❑ Have worked as a volunteer for the Republicans, especially if you're a Democrat.

❑ Know what to do if you receive a jury summons or a subpoena to appear at a trial.

❑ Have observed an open civil trial, choosing a case relevant to your professional interests.

❑ Have observed an open criminal trial, choosing a case relevant to your personal interests.

❑ Have read differing accounts of the same famous trial, written by advocates of the opposing sides, and paid close attention to their attempts at persuasion, whether worthy or not.

❑ Know the difference between a misdemeanor and a felony and how their punishments differ.

❑ Know about the appeals process, especially in the case of the most serious crimes.

❑ Know how to talk to the police when stopped or questioned, especially if you are in the wrong.

❑ Know your rights if arrested and the name of an attorney you can call in an emergency.

❑ Have made friends with your local police and participated in community activities to help them.

❑ Have toured a local fire station, tried on a hat, and asked how you can help prevent fires.

❑ Know and always respect any community curfews for people of your age.

❑ Have the nerve to contest a traffic violation in court (if you think you were in the right), or to report a bus driver or cabdriver to the authorities (if you believe he or she was driving unsafely), or to otherwise exercise your rights as a citizen in similar ways.

❑ Know your rights—and especially your responsibilities—as a pedestrian and as a bicyclist.

❑ Know your local energy- and water-conservation laws so that you don't participate in wasteful practices.

❑ Know how to recycle according to the law in your community and why such laws are necessary.

❑ Know your local litter laws and pollution laws so that you don't violate them unknowingly.

❑ Have volunteered to participate in a community-beautification program.

❑ Have volunteered your services to help in a local emergency, such as a flood.

❑ Have helped gather food and clothing for needy families and individuals at both special times (such as holidays) and occasionally during the rest of the year.

❑ Have found a way to make a significant personal contribution to the continuing improvement in race relations in our country.

EXTRA CREDIT

Have run for a student office regularly, in both grade school and high school, regardless of whether you thought you had a prayer of getting elected.

Resources

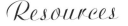

Following are the names and contact information for organizations that may be helpful in your efforts to achieve your goals. Don't hesitate to get in touch with them.

American Alliance for Health, Physical Education, Recreation and Dance
1900 Association Drive
Reston, VA 20191-1598
(800) 213-7193
Fax: (703) 476-9527
E-mail: aahperd@aahperd.org
www.aahperd.org

The American Alliance for Health, Physical Education, Recreation and Dance is a group whose mission is to support creative and healthy lifestyles through programs in health, physical education, recreation, dance and sport.

American Astronomical Society
2000 Florida Avenue NW
Suite 400
Washington, DC 20009-1231
(202) 328-2010
Fax: (202) 234-2560
E-mail: aas@aas.org
www.aas.org

The American Astronomical Society was formed in 1899 and is the major North American professional organization for astronomers, other scientists, and individuals interested in astronomy.

American Camping Association
5000 State Road 67 North
Martinsville, IN 46151-7902
(765) 342-8456
Fax: (765) 342-2065
www.acacamps.org

The American Camping Association (ACA) is an organization of camp professionals who work together to ensure the quality of camps and camp programs. The group accredits camps that meet their health, safety, and program-quality standards.

American Chemical Society
1155 Sixteenth Street NW
Washington, DC 20036
(800) 227-5558 (US only)
(202) 872-4540 (outside US)
Fax: (202) 776-8258
E-mail: webmaster@acs.org
www.acs.org

The American Chemical Society works to promote public perception and understanding of chemistry. The organization also maintains the Chem Abstracts Service, the world's largest database of chemical information.

American Council for the Arts

1 East 53rd Street
New York, NY 10022-4201
(212) 223-2787
Fax: (212) 980-4857
www.artsusa.org

The American Council for the Arts conducts research, organizes conferences, publishes books and periodicals, and advocates public policies that advance the contribution of the arts and artists to American life.

American Craft Council

72 Spring Street
New York, NY 10012
(212) 274-0630
Fax: (212) 274-0650
E-mail: council@craftcouncil.org
www.craftcouncil.org

The American Craft Council is a nonprofit educational organization dedicated to creating an environment in which craft is understood and appreciated. The council is a membership organization that welcomes those with an interest in or curiosity about crafts.

American Medical Association

515 North State Street
Chicago, IL 60610
(312) 464-5000
www.ama-assn.org

The American Medical Association is an organization composed of professional physicians who promote the science and art of medicine to improve public health. At their Website, patients can find helpful information on how to find a new doctor, a new hospital, and up-to-date medical information.

American Society for the Prevention of Cruelty to Animals

424 East 92nd Street
New York, NY 10128
(212) 876-7700
www.aspca.org

The American Society for the Prevention of Cruelty to Animals promotes humane principles and works to prevent mistreatment of animals. The organization also provides information on pet adoption, pet care, and local animal shelters.

Boy Scouts of America

National Council
PO Box 152079
Irving, TX 75015-2079
For more information, please contact your local council.
www.bsa.scouting.org

The National Council of the Boy Scouts of America supports more than three hundred local councils that provide youth programs, including Tiger Cubs, Cub Scouting, Boy Scouting and Venturing. Boys between the ages of seven and twenty may join a scouting program. Scouting provides boys with opportunities to build character, learn citizenship skills, and train to become physically and mentally fit through a variety of activities.

The Children's Defense Fund

25 E Street NW
Washington, DC 20001
(202) 628-8787
E-mail: cdfinfo@childrensdefense.org

The mission of the Children's Defense Fund (CDF) is to ensure that every child gets a safe, fair, healthy, and moral start in life to help him or her become an adult with the community's support. The organization advocates for children who cannot lobby for themselves and educates the public on what children need to help them succeed in the future.

Corporation for National Service

1201 New York Avenue NW
Washington, DC 20525
(202) 606-5000
E-mail: webmaster@cns.gov
www.nationalservice.org

The Corporation for National Service provides information on and opportunities to volunteer in your community and abroad. The Corporation also runs AmeriCorps, which provides persons seventeen and older with the chance to earn money toward their education while volunteering.

Council of Better Business Bureaus
4200 Wilson Boulevard
Suite 800
Arlington, VA 22203-1838
(703) 276-0100
Fax: (703) 525-8277
www.bbb.org

Founded in 1912, the Better Business Bureau system is dedicated to fostering fair and honest relationships between businesses and consumers through voluntary self-regulation, consumer and business education, and service excellence.

4-H Council
7100 Connecticut Avenue
Chevy Chase, MD 20815
(301) 961-2800
E-mail: info@fourhcouncil.edu
www.4-h.org

Maintained by the U.S. Department of Agriculture, the National 4-H Council is an organization designed to promote an environment in which young people learn, grow and work together to effect positive changes in the world around them. Youths ages five to nineteen can become members and meet new people while learning life skills and responsibility.

Girl Scouts of America
420 Fifth Avenue
New York, NY 10018-2798
(800) 478-7248
www.gsusa.org or www.girlscouts.org

The world's largest organization for girls, with almost four million members, the Girl Scouts of the USA is open to all girls ages five to seventeen. Scouting enables girls to have fun and make friends while developing life skills.

International Food Information Council Foundation
1100 Connecticut Avenue NW
Suite 430
Washington, DC 20036
(202) 296-6540
Fax: (202) 296-6547
E-mail: foodinfo@ificinfo.health.org
www.ificinfo.health.org

The International Food Information Council is a nonprofit educational organization designed to disseminate science-based information on health, nutrition, and food safety for the public good.

MoterVoter.com
www.motorvoter.com

This site explains the origins of the National Voter Registration Act of 1993 and provides updates, facts, and statistics relating to this piece of legislation. The site also allows one to access a mail-in voter-registration form that can be used to register to vote. (Please note that Minnesota, North Dakota, Wyoming, and Wisconsin are exempt from the 1993 act).

National Association for Gifted Children
1707 L Street NW
Suite 550
Washington, DC 20036
(202) 785-4268
Fax: (202) 785-4248
www.nagc.org

The National Association for Gifted Children is a nonprofit organization comprised of parents, teachers, professionals, and community leaders that addresses the needs of children with demonstrated talents, as well as those children able to further their talent with educational experiences. NAGC works to improve education quality for all students in collaboration with other organizations and agencies.

National Council on Economic Education

1140 Avenue of the Americas
New York, NY 10036
(800) 338-1192
E-mail: info@ncee.net
www.nationalcouncil.org

The National Council on Economic Education (NCEE) is a nonprofit group of education, business, and labor leaders dedicated to helping young people learn to function in today's world economy. The council seeks to improve economic literacy and understanding from kindergarten to college and beyond.

National Council on Family Relations

3989 Central Avenue NE
Suite 550
Minneapolis, MN 55421
(888) 781-9331
Fax: (763) 781-9348
E-mail: info@ncfr.org
www.ncfr.org

The National Council on Family Relations provides a forum for family researchers, educators, and practitioners to share and disseminate knowledge of families and family relationships. The council also establishes professional standards and works to promote family well-being.

National Federation of Music Clubs

1336 North Delaware Street
Indianapolis, IN 46202
(317) 638-4003
(806) 799-4160 (for information on auditions)
www.nfmc-music.org

The National Federation of Music Clubs is the world's largest philanthropic music organization. The Federation supports American music and musicians of all ages by offering opportunities to study and perform and by sponsoring annual competitions with cash awards.

National Safety Council

1121 Spring Lake Drive
Itasca, IL 61043-3201
(630) 285-1121
Fax: (630) 285-1315
www.nsc.org

The National Safety Council is an international nonprofit public-service organization dedicated to improving the health, safety, and environmental well-being of all people. The council's library contains valuable safety and health information resources.

Sierra Club

85 Second Street
Second Floor
San Francisco, CA 94105-3441
(415) 977-5500
Fax: (415) 977-5799
E-mail: information@sierraclub.org
www.sierraclub.org

The Sierra Club is an environmental organization whose members practice and promote the responsible use of the earth's ecosystems and resources. The club educates people on how to protect and restore the quality of the natural environment, so as to preserve it for the use and appreciation of future generations.

Toastmasters International

PO Box 9052
Mission Viejo, CA 92690
(949) 858-8255
Fax: 949-858-1207
www.toastmasters.org

Toastmasters International is a nonprofit organization dedicated to improving public speaking, leadership, and listening skills. Each Toastmaster club consists of twenty to thirty people who meet once a week to practice conducting meetings, presenting speeches (both impromptu and prepared), and offering constructive evaluations.

About the Author

Marilyn vos Savant is a national columnist. Since 1986, she has been writing the "Ask Marilyn" column for *Parade*, the Sunday magazine distributed by 349 newspapers in all fifty states, with a circulation of 37.1 million and a readership of 80 million, the largest in the world. She is also an executive at Jarvik Heart, Inc., which manufactures artificial hearts for temporary and permanent use in the treatment of heart failure.

Vos Savant was listed in the *Guinness Book of World Records* for five years under "Highest I.Q." for both her childhood and adult scores. She has since been inducted into the Guinness Hall of Fame. Vos Savant was named by Toastmasters as the No. 1 most-popular communicator/speaker in the educational and social category in 2000. She was named one of fifty "Women of the New Millennium" by the *Vital Voices: Women in Democracy* campaign of the White House in 2001.

She serves on the Board of Directors of the National Council on Economic Education, is a member of the Advisory Board for the National Association for Gifted Children, and is a member of the Advisory Board for the National Women's History Museum.

Vos Savant appeared on the weekly "Ask Marilyn" question-and-answer segment for the evening news on WCBS, the New York affiliate for the CBS network, and her stage play *Poppa's*

Will was produced Off-Off-Broadway. Another play is in the works.

Marilyn vos Savant was born in St. Louis, Missouri, the daughter of Mary vos Savant and Joseph Mach (granddaughter of Mary Savant and Joseph vos Savant; granddaughter of Anna Moravec and Anton Mach). She is married to Robert Jarvik, M.D., inventor of the Jarvik 7 and Jarvik 2000 artificial hearts, and has two grown children, Mary and Denny. She and her husband reside in Manhattan.